MW00337741

Student-Centered Coaching From a Distance

LIBRARY OF
CONGRESS
SURPLUS
DUPLICATE

This book is dedicated to the instructional coaches, teachers,
and leaders who have taught us so much over the past year.
We thank those who contributed to this book and all the others
who shared their personal experiences, which helped inform our thinking.

As Buddha says, "every experience, no matter how bad it seems,
holds within it a blessing of some kind. The goal is to find it." We have
found that blessing through each and every one of you. Thank you.

Student-Centered Coaching From a Distance

Coaching Moves for Virtual, Hybrid, and In-Person Classrooms

Diane Sweeney

Leanna S. Harris

FOR INFORMATION:

Corwin

A SAGE Company

2455 Teller Road

Thousand Oaks, California 91320

(800) 233-9936

www.corwin.com

SAGE Publications Ltd.

1 Oliver's Yard

55 City Road

London EC1Y 1SP

United Kingdom

SAGE Publications India Pvt. Ltd.

B 1/I 1 Mohan Cooperative Industrial Area

Mathura Road, New Delhi 110 044

India

SAGE Publications Asia-Pacific Pte. Ltd.

18 Cross Street #10-10/11/12

China Square Central

Singapore 048423

Program Director and Publisher: Dan Alpert

Senior Content
  Development Editor: Lucas Schleicher

Associate Content
  Development Editor: Mia Rodriguez

Production Editor: Megha Negi

Copy Editor: Laureen Gleason

Typesetter: C&M Digitals (P) Ltd.

Proofreader: Eleni-Maria Georgiou

Indexer: Integra

Cover Designer: Candice Harman

Marketing Manager: Sharon Pendergast

Copyright © 2021 by Corwin Press, Inc.

All rights reserved. Except as permitted by U.S. copyright law, no part of this work may be reproduced or distributed in any form or by any means, or stored in a database or retrieval system, without permission in writing from the publisher.

When forms and sample documents appearing in this work are intended for reproduction, they will be marked as such. Reproduction of their use is authorized for educational use by educators, local school sites, and/or noncommercial or nonprofit entities that have purchased the book.

All third party trademarks referenced or depicted herein are included solely for the purpose of illustration and are the property of their respective owners. Reference to these trademarks in no way indicates any relationship with, or endorsement by, the trademark owner.

Printed in the United States of America

Library of Congress Cataloging-in-Publication Data

Names: Sweeney, Diane, author. | Harris, Leanna, author.

Title: Student-centered coaching from a distance : coaching moves for virtual, hybrid, and in-person classrooms / Diane Sweeney, Leanna S. Harris.

Description: Thousand Oaks, California : Corwin, [2021] | Includes bibliographical references and index.

Identifiers: LCCN 2020054412 | ISBN 9781071845370 (paperback) | ISBN 9781071845387 (epub) | ISBN 9781071845400 (epub) | ISBN 9781071845431 (pdf)

Subjects: LCSH: Student-centered learning—Study and teaching. | Effective teaching. | Mentoring in education. | Education—Computer assisted instruction.

Classification: LCC LB1027.23 .S95 2021 | DDC 371.39—dc23

LC record available at https://lccn.loc.gov/2020054412

This book is printed on acid-free paper.

20 21 22 23 24 10 9 8 7 6 5 4 3 2 1

DISCLAIMER: This book may direct you to access third-party content via web links, QR codes, or other scannable technologies, which are provided for your reference by the author(s). Corwin makes no guarantee that such third-party content will be available for your use and encourages you to review the terms and conditions of such third-party content. Corwin takes no responsibility and assumes no liability for your use of any third-party content, nor does Corwin approve, sponsor, endorse, verify, or certify such third-party content.

Contents

Visit the companion website at
http://resources.corwin.com/SCCFromaDistance
for downloadable resources.

List of Figures

About the Authors

Diane Sweeney is the author of *The Essential Guide for Student-Centered Coaching* (Corwin, 2020), *Leading Student-Centered Coaching* (Corwin, 2018), and *Student-Centered Coaching: The Moves* (Corwin, 2017). Each of these books is grounded in the simple but powerful premise that coaching can be designed to more directly impact student learning.

Diane spends her time speaking and consulting for schools and educational organizations across the country. She is also an instructor for the University of Wisconsin–Madison. When she isn't working in schools, she loves to spend time outside with her family in Denver, Colorado.

Leanna S. Harris is the author of *The Essential Guide for Student-Centered Coaching* (Corwin, 2020) and *Student-Centered Coaching: The Moves* (Corwin, 2017). She has worked as a teacher, coach, and consultant across Grades K–12 and currently works with Diane Sweeney Consulting to help schools and districts implement Student-Centered Coaching. Her work is based on the belief that professional development for teachers is most effective when it is grounded in outcomes for student achievement—for every child, every day.

Leanna is a passionate skier and cyclist. She lives in Denver, Colorado with her husband and three kids.

Introduction

The online/distance-learning curve has everyone climbing uphill in our district. Even some of our best teachers are struggling to ensure that their targets are clear, that the technology they choose to use is being utilized effectively, and that their most vulnerable students are truly learning. Some are not open to coaching right now because their confidence is low regarding virtual learning. They are just trying to keep their heads above water.

—Sheryl Bibby, District Coach, Louisville, Kentucky

WHO KNEW?

Who knew that in 2020, schools would close in mid-March? Who could have imagined teachers working from home? Who hasn't shed tears hearing how hard teachers are working to do right by their students? The answer, of course, is that none of us knew. The cognitive dissonance has been extreme, but as the months roll on, we are beginning to be able to peer into the rearview mirror to find lessons, strategies, and ways of being that will likely persist well beyond COVID-19. Sure, right now, we may still be in the third or fourth inning (who really knows), but what we know is that educators will always innovate through challenging situations. This is no different.

There is no question that teachers are facing unprecedented challenges as they adjust to hybrid or virtual instruction. Many proven pedagogical practices have been difficult to implement in these formats, which means we must constantly adapt our strategies for teaching and learning. As coaches, we must also shift our practices to remain student-centered and respond to the needs of students and teachers at the same time. We believe that today, teachers need coaching more than ever.

IT'S A MATTER OF EQUITY

Tragically, the equity gap continues to expand as our students and their families face unstable housing, food, and schooling. In Aurora Public Schools in Colorado, for example, more than 1.8 million pounds of food have been distributed to families, and this is barely putting a dent in the needs within the community. It may feel like an avalanche of need, because it is. But that doesn't mean we can't contribute as instructional coaches.

Throughout this book, we strive to connect Student-Centered Coaching with practices that promote equity. This includes coaching at a distance in virtual, hybrid, and in-person settings. We do not kid ourselves by thinking that instructional coaching provides all the answers to the equity issues in our schools. What we do know is that Student-Centered Coaching creates the opportunity to work together to remove many of the classroom equity barriers through coaching conversations.

As our friend and fellow coach Brooke O'Drobinak likes to say, "equity and coaching are dancing partners." If we hope to respond to the teaching and learning needs that COVID-19 has surfaced, we must respond to the persistent needs around equity as well. They are one and the same.

WHAT IS STUDENT-CENTERED COACHING?

Student-Centered Coaching is an evidence-based coaching model. Rather than hoping that coaching will impact student learning, that's what our approach is designed to do. We ask teachers what they would like their students to learn, and then we co-plan and co-teach to get them there. This allows us to impact teaching and learning at the same time.

As we wrote about in *The Essential Guide for Student-Centered Coaching* (Sweeney & Harris, 2020), we operate from the following guiding principles that serve as the philosophical underpinnings for Student-Centered Coaching. They are at the heart of our beliefs about coaching. As you read the list, we invite you to consider which of the following principles are still relevant, given the times we are in. (The answer, of course, is all of them.)

- Coaching is not about "fixing" teachers.
- Coaching is a partnership focused on student learning.
- Coaching is about continual professional growth.
- Coaching is part of a robust ecosystem of professional learning.

The question for many instructional coaches has been "How can I adapt to the current environment while staying true to Student-Centered Coaching?" Answering this question is what this book is about. Each chapter will include a series of "moves" you can make as an instructional coach. These moves are accompanied by tools such as language, checklists, protocols, and other resources that provide structure and coherence to coaching conversations. As always, we invite you to use these tools as a launching-off point. Never hesitate to adapt them to meet your needs; they are here for you. We have also included firsthand experiences from a number of coaches who are out there right now doing their best to figure it all out. Just like you. Just like us.

Let's get started.

CHAPTER 1

Keep the Focus on Student Learning

Unsure of what to expect in this new environment, my best guess was that teachers would primarily want to know about shifts in pacing and new resources. What I found is they craved coaching more than ever! Someone to think through how best to meet the needs of their students was the repeated plea from nearly every teacher I encountered.

—Stacey Shamis, Title I Coach

We were all stunned when COVID-19 began affecting our schools. Quetzal, a middle schooler in Wisconsin, described it like this: "On March 12, some of our teachers were frantically telling us to clear out our lockers because we might not be back. Others were saying we'd be back the next Monday. No one knew what was going on. It was crazy!" As the confusion persisted, districts began distributing computers and hotspots while teachers transitioned their lessons online. During this time, many coaches felt they had very little control over what they could (or should) be doing to help. Proximity to teachers, one of a coach's strongest assets, was taken away as we all began working from home. Many coaches felt like teachers had so much on their plates that they wouldn't want to be bothered. We were all unmoored and unsure of what we should be doing from day to day.

At the beginning, coaches found that they were doing whatever it took to help everyone survive. Very little of the focus was on student learning, which was illustrated by the fact that many districts established no-grading policies. As the months have progressed, things have gotten better. Yet it is also becoming evident that this is going to last a while, and we may be shifting between virtual and in-person learning for many months to come.

MOVE 1: CONTINUE TO COACH IN A WAY THAT'S STUDENT-CENTERED

Because COVID-19 has disproportionately affected our underserved populations, certain schools are finding that it is more of a struggle to return to "normal." Take Denver Public Schools as an example. Several years ago, the district moved to a choice-based enrollment model, which means that today, students don't necessarily attend their neighborhood school but are dispersed throughout the city. Couple that with the fact that the transportation offered for high school students is a city bus pass, which now is limiting ridership. Even though the district wants to return to in-person instruction, it turns out that one of the biggest barriers it's facing is getting these students to school.

With such profound challenges, it is easy to overlook the power of coaching. It's also easy to get overwhelmed and wonder where we fit in as coaches. We understand that there has been some need for teachers to adapt, but we will also continue to advocate for coaching on behalf of our students. We can be a part of the solution, no matter whether schools are virtual, hybrid, or in-person.

HOW CAN WE STAY STUDENT-CENTERED?

When describing different approaches to coaching, we use the language of relationship-driven, teacher-centered, and student-centered coaching to frame what we've seen as we have supported coaches over the past few decades. Figure 1.1 details the role, focus, use of data, and other common coaching behaviors for each approach.

We like to think of this figure as a dartboard. While we continually aim for the center, which is student learning, it doesn't mean that we won't hit the outer rings at certain

FIGURE 1.1 ● Student-Centered, Teacher-Centered, and Relationship-Driven Coaching

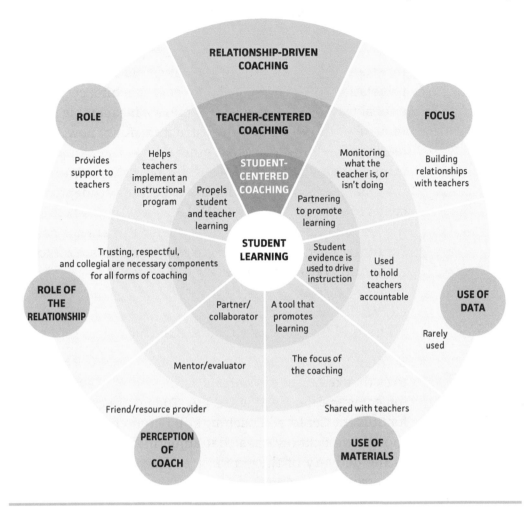

Source: Sweeney, D., and Harris, L. (2020). *The Essential Guide for Student-Centered Coaching*. Reprinted with permission.

times, especially in the current landscape of schools. The key is to aim our attention toward student learning as much of the time as possible.

How we accomplish this can happen in many different ways. While we have emphasized coaching cycles in the past (and we still believe in them), they aren't the only structure we can use to have student-centered conversations with teachers. This year has been hard on coaches who hold themselves to a high bar and measure their value based solely on implementing coaching cycles. We certainly celebrate this approach, but we'd like to point out that coaching cycles actually aren't on the bullseye in Figure 1.1. Rather, when describing Student-Centered Coaching, we focus on using student evidence, creating partnerships, using materials as a tool for student learning, and developing trusting and respectful relationships with teachers. While coaching cycles are a critical way to coach deeply and make a measurable impact, remember that they are only a structure. Right now, it might feel more realistic to coach in other ways—for example, with mini coaching cycles, lesson planning, unit planning, and informal support. What matters is keeping students at the center of every conversation. We know we'll get back to broad implementation of coaching cycles when this era has passed. For those coaches who are there now, our hats are off to you for finding ways to coach deeply.

CORE PRACTICES FOR STUDENT-CENTERED COACHING

Student-Centered Coaching is driven by a set of core practices that keep student learning at the center of every coaching conversation (see Figure 1.2). Today, the core practices for Student-Centered Coaching still remain front and center, though we acknowledge that adjustments must be made in the delivery of these practices for virtual, hybrid, and in-person classrooms.

FIGURE 1.2 ● Core Practices for Student-Centered Coaching

1	2	3	4	5	6	7
Utilize coaching cycles	Set standards-based goals	Unpack the goal into learning targets	Co-plan with student evidence	Co-teach using effective instructional practices	Measure the impact on student and teacher learning	Partner with the school leader

The first core practice is to utilize **coaching cycles**. Coaching cycles are how we ensure that coaching makes a lasting impact. As we just mentioned, it may take longer to get coaching cycles up and running in the current situation, as many teachers are on extreme learning curves regarding technology and curriculum, but we still want to get there eventually. To learn more about coaching cycles, check out Chapter 2 in *The Essential Guide for Student-Centered Coaching* (Sweeney & Harris, 2020).

Another approach is mini coaching cycles, which will be introduced in Chapter 2 of this book as a way to stay student-centered and allow teachers a bit of space and time to become fully immersed in coaching. Mini coaching cycles share the same attributes as full cycles but are narrower in focus and shorter in duration. While most mini coaching cycles are rooted in the standards, they are also a good place to work with teachers on goals related to engagement, process, or language acquisition.

Full coaching cycles begin with a **standards-based goal** for student learning. This is because we align our coaching cycles with a unit of study and spend several weeks working side by side to ensure that the students reach the goal. This practice keeps us at the center of the bullseye because it ensures that we are focusing on teaching and learning. In today's context, teachers are still responsible for teaching the standards. Whether inside or outside of a school building, students are there to learn, and this is where we must keep our focus.

Distance learning requires students to be more independent and self-paced in their learning. Right now, students may physically be in the school a few days a week or not at all. When they aren't on campus, we must create the conditions for our students to be able to move themselves through the learning. The core practice of **using learning targets** supports students in navigating these new demands.

By developing a set of learning targets, we provide success criteria that students can use to progress through their learning with a clear sense of what they're expected to accomplish. To make this happen, the learning targets are student-friendly, so that student goal setting and self-assessment can take place. Each coaching conversation is anchored in the learning targets because they provide a clear path toward the expected student outcomes. With this information in hand, the teacher(s) and coach are in a better position to co-plan and co-teach lessons across the coaching cycle.

Co-planning with student evidence is a hallmark of Student-Centered Coaching. While the student evidence in a virtual setting may look different than it does in an in-person class-room, it is still a vital part of the process. We recommend that coaches work with teachers to identify tech tools that are formative in nature and surface where the students are as learners. This includes using applications such as Padlet, Jamboard, Flipgrid, Google Forms, and others. When these tools are used in a formative manner, they can inform instructional planning, just like the assessments that we have used in the past have done. In Chapter 4, we will take a close look at the practices that can be used for co-planning units and lessons with teachers.

Co-teaching also looks different in a virtual setting. We may not be able to walk down the hallway to join lessons like we used to. If school is being held in person, there may be only a portion (or cohort) of students present, or students may be spread out for social distancing. Even though it might not feel like it, there are rich opportunities for coaches to join lessons from a distance and contribute and collaborate with teachers. Chapter 5 will provide moves to do just that.

One of the reasons we advocate for utilizing coaching cycles is so that we can **measure the impact** of coaching on teaching and learning. This core practice involves using the Results-Based Coaching Tool to collect data across a coaching cycle. While the assessments we use may need to be adjusted, this core practice still applies. In Resource A of this book, you'll find a template of the Results-Based Coaching Tool, along with an annotated version.

The last core practice is to **partner with the school leader**. Without a solid principal–coach partnership, the coach will not be able to make the desired impact. It is more important than ever to clearly define roles and create systems for coaching in a virtual context. This will be addressed in Chapter 7 as we strive to facilitate strong partnerships with the principal and others across schools.

COACH AS RESOURCE PROVIDER

With the sudden shift to remote learning, many coaches initially spent their time serving as resource providers. This included helping teachers set up online libraries, figuring out the learning management system (LMS), and making sure that students had access to the necessary technology. At the time, this made sense, given what teachers were facing. The issue arises when this is the *only* role that a coach plays. This may diminish the impact of the coaching program, because these forms of support are not anchored in enhancing student learning.

Another way coaches served as resource providers was by providing tech support that was more about the technology and less about student learning. For many years, tech coaches have tried to assert that their role shouldn't be limited to this function, yet it became all the more common with the current technology demands.

Much of this involved coaches working with teachers to create online substitutes for existing lessons, even though best practices in educational technology (EdTech) remind us that this is only the first level of technology integration. A conceptual tool that represents this is known as the SAMR Model (see Figure 1.3). If coaches focus only on helping teachers create substitute lessons, they are missing opportunities to redefine what learning might look like for students.

It's a fine line when carving out a role in coaching around technology. We don't want to get trapped helping with surface support in the use of technology, and we don't want to become too teacher-centered, either. If we think of our primary role as being about student learning first and the creation of transformative lessons second, we are coaching to our full potential.

FIGURE 1.3 ● The SAMR Model

THE SAMR MODEL

Dr. Ruben R. Puentedura

S **SUBSTITUTION**
Technology acts as a direct substitute, with no functional change

A **AUGMENTATION**
Technology acts as a direct substitute, with functional improvement

M **MODIFICATION**
Technology allows for significant task redesign

R **REDEFINITION**
Technology allows for the creation of new tasks, previously inconceivable

ENHANCEMENT

TRANSFORMATION

Source: Explanation of the SAMR Model created by Lefflerd, 3 April 2016: https://commons.wikimedia.org/wiki/File:The_SAMR_Model.jpg. Licensed under CC BY-SA 4.0: https://creativecommons.org/licenses/by-sa/4.0/

A strategy to avoid getting stuck for too long as resource providers is to allow ourselves a few weeks at the beginning of the year (or during a transition, such as the closing of schools) to serve in this role and then put a date on the calendar for when to shift to more student-centered work. This creates some accountability without too much pressure. We also recommend that principals and coaches closely analyze how they are spending their time. This can be achieved through time audits and calendar reviews. If a coach isn't doing work that directly impacts student and teacher learning for too long, it's time to make some adjustments in their coaching practice.

Tool: How Have I Been Spending My Time as a Coach?

As you consider your coaching practice, how balanced has your work been? Put a check next to the statements that represent how you have been mostly spending your time as a coach. If you have more than a few checks, you may be ready to move beyond being a resource provider.

- ❑ I am mostly helping teachers with support, such as organizing assessments or other clerical duties.
- ❑ I am mostly helping teachers get technology systems in place.
- ❑ I am mostly engaged in conversations that are one-shot or drive-by.
- ❑ I am mostly working behind the scenes to write lessons and units for the teachers.
- ❑ I am mostly covering classes so that my school can manage cohorts of students.

DISPATCH FROM THE FIELD

Amy Garrett, Educational Technology Coach

When I arrived at the Hong Kong International School as a tech coach in 2019, I was immediately charged with equipping, setting up, and rolling out a brand-new makerspace. Much of my first few months were spent physically setting up the space, which was essentially a shell with a random assortment of donated supplies. I spent a lot of time and energy inviting teachers and classes into the space for lessons I designed and led. I loved what I was doing, but I'd hardly say I was coaching.

Cue COVID-19 hitting Hong Kong in early January 2020. I was suddenly catapulted into emergency IT triage. Seemingly overnight, we shifted into virtual learning—no prep, no pause. I played a central role in developing and establishing our school's home-learning platforms and approach. While I appreciated the trust and responsibility from my administrators, as well as the leadership experience, it was pedal to the metal from day one.

As the tech coach, I was leading PD, creating websites, and developing platform agreements and documents to support our school's home-learning program. Teachers were at varying levels of comfort and ability with technology, so I was doing all sorts of mundane IT support tasks as well: making learning grid Google Doc templates, checking links, posting on the websites, troubleshooting tech. I knew my role as a coach was to be there when teachers needed me and to encourage even the most experienced teachers as their foundations were rocked. We are blessed to have a fairly tech-savvy staff, but it's safe to say none of us were fully prepared for this massive shift in approach to teaching and learning.

(Continued)

(Continued)

During this time, I forged impressively strong connections and relationships with my new colleagues out of intense necessity. I built trust and respected their vulnerability—supporting without judgment and building them up little by little in individual ways. Looking back, I feel this has been a silver lining amid all the tragedy and loss of the pandemic. In normal times, it would have taken far longer to have made those contact points with every colleague while working to build an understanding and culture of coaching. Many were stunned this August, when I reminded them that it was just my second year at the school; we all felt as if we had been through years of teaching together.

The start of this school year still found me providing tech support, but with far less frequency or sense of urgency. This has allowed me to shift the focus of my role from specialist and IT support to a true technology coach. The trusting relationships that were built in the spring have paved the way for meaningful conversations about how to successfully use technology to transform learning experiences. We have a long way to go, but we have already come far. In the midst of all the chaos, disappointment, and frustration the pandemic has brought, I'm grateful for the way it has positively shaped my role and highlighted the importance, value, and necessity of instructional coaches in schools.

FOCUSING ON STUDENT LEARNING PROMOTES EQUITY

Learning loss as a result of the pandemic is creating gaps that especially affect our most vulnerable students. This includes second-language learners, students with learning differences, and those who have been victims of structural racism, such as our Black and Native American students. Having taught and coached in these communities for many years, we've witnessed the lack of resources and support that often exists. COVID-19 has only made things worse.

If we are strategic, coaching can play a role in filling these gaps. As educators, we must be hypervigilant about monitoring our students of concern. Coaches can help carry the load by working with teachers to formatively assess and create plans for the students we are striving to serve. This doesn't mean we add to the bureaucracy by inundating these students with assessments and data collection that don't tell us a whole lot about what they need as learners *right now*. Cornelius Minor (2019) notes that if we turn students into data points, they lose their personhood. More testing runs the risk of dehumanizing our students. This is why we deliberately use the term *student evidence* rather than *data*, because it refers to the thinking, writing, and reading that the students are producing every day. By helping teachers build intentional relationships with their students, we facilitate the creation of a close-up view of how they are progressing as learners and what additional support they might need. This notion of inclusion reaches far beyond sending students down the hall for additional services. Our job is to know students as learners so that we can work with teachers to design a path forward for each and every one.

We can also promote equity by fostering collective teacher efficacy. According to John Hattie's (2019) work on Visible Learning influences, collective teacher efficacy has the largest effect size to date ($d = 1.39$). Donohoo (2017) writes, "When teachers believe that together they and their colleagues can impact student achievement, they share a sense of collective teacher efficacy. Collective efficacy is high when teachers believe that the staff is capable of helping students master complex content, fostering students' creativity, and getting students to believe they can do well in school" (p. 3). One of the most important jobs for coaches is to help teachers believe they can have a positive impact on all students.

This means that we work with teachers to create meaningful formative assessments, co-plan high-quality lessons that meet the needs of all students, and foster an overall belief that students can get there when we work together to provide them with choice, voice, and agency. This enables students to become not only partners in the learning process but also key navigators of their own learning. Working with teachers to provide students with choice, voice, and agency is certainly challenging in an online learning environment, but it can be done. We'll explore this further in Chapter 6.

MOVE 2: BUILD RELATIONSHIPS FROM A DISTANCE

When everyone feels known and engaged, it ripples through the entire school. When we feel welcomed, accepted, and safe, we are ready to show up and contribute to the broader community. You may be wondering how a coach can contribute to this lofty goal. One way is to truly know people—all people. We aren't implying that you need to know everything about everybody. It might simply be milestones, like the teacher who just had a grandbaby or the family that just adopted a new puppy. It could also be the challenges students are facing, such as those who may be caretaking for siblings while participating in online school. To know is to forge connections and belonging. To describe this, Stephanie Leonard-Witte, assistant superintendent in Sun Prairie Schools (Wisconsin), uses the phrase "by name and by face" in conversations within her district. "By name and by face" has become a mantra for building meaningful relationships with every member of the school community. This includes students, teachers, families, support staff, and administrators. She believes that until we are able to truly know others, we will fail to create a pathway to true connection, learning, and equity.

Opportunities to make connections are rooted in our being curious about the stories of other people. We can listen and say, "Tell me more. . . ." Some coaches keep a journal of the connections they are making with others. This creates the opportunity to reach out to a few more people each week. For those of us who aren't the best at remembering names, it can be helpful to come up with a system, such as a staff roster with photos. We recognize that making these types of connections is more challenging at a distance, but it can be done.

Successful coaching is built on trusting relationships with teachers. Successful teaching is built on trusting relationships with our students. This has always been important, but today, the lack of connection we are experiencing due to the shift away from in-person school has created a sense of loss and disorientation for many students, teachers, coaches, and school leaders. When trusting relationships are in place, it becomes much easier to keep coaching conversations focused on student learning. Working with teachers to create connection and belonging in their classrooms is one of the most meaningful roles we can play right now as a coach.

HOW TO CREATE BELONGING IN THE CLASSROOM

> When students fail to connect with their instructor or with their classmates, they disengage. This disengagement results in lower attendance, lower assignment completion, and lower achievement. In other words, by every metric imaginable, students learn less and perform worse when they aren't connecting with others. (Spencer, 2020, para. 4)

If we create an environment where our students feel a sense of belonging, we will succeed in building relationships with students that include vulnerability, trust, and empathy. Students who sense that their teachers care about them seem to work twice as hard. And sadly, the reverse can also be true.

Partnering with teachers to reflect on the following questions helps us create classrooms in which students thrive in ways that go far beyond the lesson of the day. You may notice that while we usually use the word *we* in our coaching stems, this time we haven't. This is because we believe that it's up to the teacher to build strong relationships with their students, thus creating a classroom community—whether in-person or virtual—that will thrive throughout the school year. Our job as coaches is to help create a vision for what this might look like.

Tool: Language That Creates a Sense of Belonging Among Students

- When you envision your classroom community, what do you hope it will feel like for each of your students?

- What specific steps will you take to engage students who haven't felt a sense of belonging in school?

- If school is held virtually or on a hybrid schedule, how will you build community so that all students feel connected?

- How will each student's voice be invited, honored, and valued by you and fellow students?

- What norms will be created and monitored to ensure that the students' voices are heard and honored?

- What routines will you create to allow all students to participate in the classroom community?

- As the coach, how can I support you in creating this community with your students?

MOVE 3: DETERMINE WHAT LEARNING IS ESSENTIAL

About a decade ago, the development of the Common Core Standards was a pivotal step forward to better educating students across the country. While most of us likely agree with what's included, the challenge is that there isn't enough time in the school year to teach it all. Before COVID-19, we sure did try. But now that we are facing less instructional time, we are finding this to be an impossible task. This presents a moral decision for many teachers: What do I focus on? How much time do I spend on it? Will my students be okay?

DETERMINING PRIORITY STANDARDS AT A DISTRICT LEVEL

The Fort Dodge Community School District has honed its curriculum to ensure that the priority standards are well understood throughout the district. This was a necessary step, so that teachers could get clearer on the standards, as well as where they fit within the enacted curriculum. What we appreciate about this district's approach is that it kept the process simple, led teachers through it with high-quality facilitation, and didn't expect things to move along at a linear or predictable pace. To increase clarity, the district used the following definitions from Bailey and Jakicic (2012) to guide its process:

> **Endurance:** something students will need to know for a longer period of time. These are standards that are used in a variety of units of instruction and over many years. *Example: Using context clues to understand the meaning of unknown words (a skill you can use for the rest of your life).*

> **Leverage:** standards that are taught and used in several subjects. They may even appear in more than one curricular area. *Example: Being taught to read graphs in math, which is then used in science.*

> **Readiness:** the standard prepares students for the next level of learning. These standards are prerequisite skills for future learning. *Example: Kindergarten students are taught letter-sound recognition because it is a necessary skill to learn to read.*

The following protocol details how the district went about this work.

TOOL: PROTOCOL FOR DETERMINING PRIORITY STANDARDS

1. Create grade or course-alike groups.

2. Provide the standards and ask participants to rank them using the rubric (see Figure 1.4).

3. Regroup and discuss the rankings. Reach consensus on which are the highest-priority standards.

4. Unwrap each of the priority standards into a set of learning targets or success criteria.

FIGURE 1.4 ● Power Standards Criteria Rubric From the Fort Dodge Community School District

	1	2	3
Endurance	The standard, if mastered, will be useful to the student in a limited number of situations.	The standard, if mastered, will be useful to the student in many situations but not necessarily all situations.	The standard, if mastered, will be useful to the student throughout life in many different situations.
Leverage	The standard, if mastered, will not help in any other disciplines or content areas.	The standard, if mastered, could be helpful in a limited number of other disciplines and content areas.	The standard, if mastered, will be useful to the student in multiple disciplines and content areas.
Readiness	The standard, if mastered, will not add to the readiness that student needs for the very next level.	The standard, if mastered, will help the student be successful at the next level, but there might be some slight gaps in the learning.	The standard, if mastered, will set the student up for success at the very next level.

Source: Created by Kirsten Doebel based on work by Ainsworth, L. (2003) and Ainsworth, L. (2004)

DETERMINING PRIORITY STANDARDS AS INDIVIDUALS OR TEAMS

Coaches may also work with individual teachers or teams to determine priority standards. This approach means we are honoring the content but also thinking about students as we determine what to focus on during instruction. It can be challenging for teachers to facilitate themselves through these conversations; hard choices must be made, because it all feels important. That's where a coach comes in. A coach can use the following questions to help teachers navigate through the decision-making process. Some of the question stems we use may seem familiar, as they are also useful for setting goals for coaching cycles. The important thing to note is that they can create pathways forward for teachers who are overwhelmed by the sheer vastness of the standards.

Tool: Language for Determining Priority Standards

- Let's look at the standards and decide which one is most relevant for your learners right now.

- Do we have any student evidence that could provide insights into what the students need?

- If we were to map the year, would this standard be revisited or only taught once?

- Is this standard used in more than one curricular area?

- Is this prerequisite learning for a future concept?

- Is this learning for all your students or a smaller group within your class?

- If you had to choose what matters most, what would it be?

- By the end of the year, what do you feel is most important for your students to know and do?

Carrie Cobb is a first-year instructional coach in Clever, Missouri, where she was a teacher for the past 17 years. Even though she already had relationships with many of her colleagues, she thought it would be a good idea to help them get to know her as a coach, especially given the unique circumstances under which they started school this year. In each chapter, you will find an e-mail message she sent to teachers during the first few weeks of school.

Message From Coach Carrie

Dear Teachers,

I am excited to be working with you this year as your K–12 Instructional Coach. My main purpose is to support and assist you in reaching your goals for student learning.

(Continued)

(Continued)

We will use state standards and district curriculum to guide these goals as we partner together to help students achieve proficiency.

In the coming weeks, I will be sending out little bits of information to give you a better understanding of how we can work together. In the meantime, feel free to contact me with any questions you may have.

In Learning,

Carrie

MOVE 4: FIND NEW WAYS TO ADDRESS GAPS

A teacher's number-one concern is that their students learn. As we moved to remote learning, teachers struggled to pinpoint how many of their students were doing, because formative assessment was harder to pull together when they couldn't collect student work at the end of class. Connections were more distant, and some students weren't engaging at all. While it can feel overwhelming, this reality presents a rich opening for coaching. When teachers ask, "How do I know if my students are learning?" we let them know that finding and addressing gaps is at the center of our coaching work. This has always been at the heart of Student-Centered Coaching, and it is no different when coaching from a distance.

A primary role for coaches is to support teachers in finding and addressing gaps between the intended goal for learning and where students are in relation to that goal. We do this by taking on the role of co-analyzer of student evidence. This allows coaches to help teachers surface, name, and act on gaps that exist. To accomplish this, we lean heavily on clear goals and learning targets in order to understand what is demanded of our students. It also means we need to formatively assess, so that we know where students are right now. We have empathy for teachers when we hear statements like "My students are so behind" or "My students don't know anything." We can contribute by responding, "Let's figure out what they can do, and then we'll plan out what we'll do next." This is an empowering stance because it's about forward thinking and action. We are no longer victims of circumstance but instead are thinking partners who are ready to envision the next step alongside teachers.

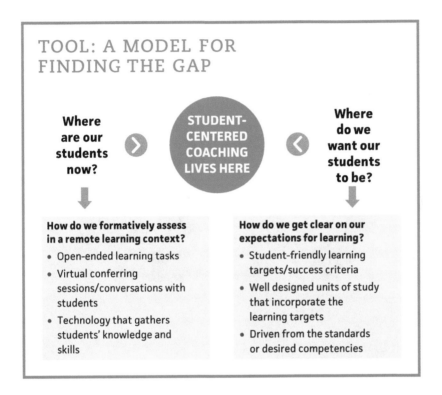

TOOL: A MODEL FOR FINDING THE GAP

Where are our students now? → STUDENT-CENTERED COACHING LIVES HERE ← **Where do we want our students to be?**

How do we formatively assess in a remote learning context?
- Open-ended learning tasks
- Virtual conferring sessions/conversations with students
- Technology that gathers students' knowledge and skills

How do we get clear on our expectations for learning?
- Student-friendly learning targets/success criteria
- Well designed units of study that incorporate the learning targets
- Driven from the standards or desired competencies

What Can We Carry Forward?

While little of what we are experiencing right now is familiar, many of the practices we have shared in this chapter are rooted in best practices for coaching, teaching, and curriculum design. We hope that as we return to "normal," we won't lose focus on things like deeply knowing our students, having a coherent and focused curriculum, and coaching from a place of formative assessment and evidence. If anything, our shared experiences remind us of the importance of these practices, and for this reason, we hope that they will endure for years to come. Here's a list of what we hope to carry into the future:

- Use technology in a way that builds connections and relationships.

- Elevate conversations about our most at-risk students.

- Narrow the focus of what we teach, so that we can go deep on what is most essential.

- Focus our coaching conversations on student learning.

CHAPTER 2

Mini Coaching Cycles

A Structure to Engage Teachers in This Moment

Coaching is exceptionally needed, but nobody has the time for it.

—Christopher L. Finch, Assistant Superintendent,
La Grange School District

Having a predictable structure for coaching is a game changer. Without a clear process, our work can feel random and unfocused. Over the years, we've tackled this through coaching cycles. Now we'd like to introduce you to mini coaching cycles. When thinking about a mini coaching cycle, it's fun to use the metaphor of a bag of potato chips. You can buy chips in party-size or lunchbox-size bags. While one is smaller than the other, they are both bags of chips. This is how we view mini coaching cycles; they consist of our foundational practices in a smaller package.

We all know that teachers are inundated right now. Some may feel like they don't have time for coaching, even when a coach could throw them the very lifeline they so desperately need. Take Rashelle as an example. Rashelle is a fourth-grade teacher who was putting in extra hours trying to design lessons that would engage her students in a unit on fractions. Rashelle went to Anita for help, and they ultimately ended up in a mini coaching cycle. As you continue reading, you'll learn how Rashelle and Anita went about this work.

WHAT IS A MINI COACHING CYCLE?

As we described in Chapter 1, Student-Centered Coaching is about partnering with teachers around goals for student learning. The structure we use for this is a coaching cycle. Coaching cycles create rich opportunities for teachers and coaches to collaborate on a standards-based goal and then monitor how the students are progressing over the four to six weeks of the cycle. We know from the work of Linda Darling-Hammond and her colleagues (2017) that professional learning needs to be focused and sustained over an extended period of time for it to have an impact on teaching practices and student learning. Yet in our current reality, we also need to be sensitive to the fact that some people may not have the bandwidth to engage in this type of deep collaboration right now. Teachers are overwhelmed with adapting to new methods of delivering instruction, the constantly changing safety guidelines, and the burgeoning social and emotional needs of their students. As instructional coaches, we want to be responsive to everything that teachers are facing, but we also understand the urgency around student outcomes. So how can we address these seemingly competing needs? We recommend mini coaching cycles as a structure that is more manageable in scope but entirely student-centered at the same time.

One great thing about mini coaching cycles is that they can be used in any of the school scenarios in which we currently find ourselves—virtual, hybrid, or in-person. Full coaching cycles go through the rotation of assess–plan–teach several times over four to six weeks, all within the context of the learning targets for the unit. However, in mini coaching cycles, we work through this sequence just once or twice. This makes mini coaching cycles shorter in duration, lasting only about one to two weeks. How long depends on the needs of the teacher and the size of the goal or target. Figure 2.1 shows how a mini coaching cycle still follows the same process as a full cycle; it's just smaller in scope.

FIGURE 2.1 ● Comparing Mini and Full Coaching Cycles

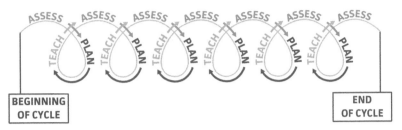

Figure 2.2 shows the stages in a mini coaching cycle, which include (1) setting the goal, (2) collecting student evidence, (3) co-planning, (4) co-teaching, and (5) reflecting and co-planning future lessons. It's helpful to keep in mind that

FIGURE 2.2 ● Stages in a Mini Coaching Cycle

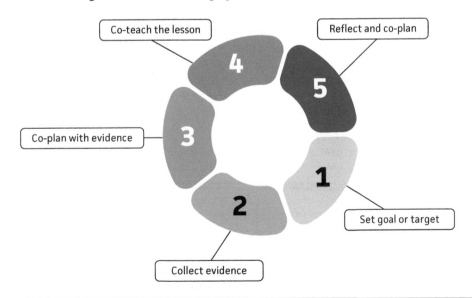

Source: Sweeney, D. and Harris, L. (2020). *The Essential Guide for Student-Centered Coaching.* Reprinted with permission.

Stages 3 and 4, co-planning and co-teaching, may happen more than once during a mini coaching cycle, depending on the needs of the teacher and students. Following each of the stages allows the coaching work to stay entirely student-centered while at the same time being of a scope and duration that may seem much more manageable to teachers right now. One more thing to note is that while full coaching cycles can occur with individuals, pairs, or small groups, mini coaching cycles are best used when collaborating with a single teacher.

DISPATCH FROM THE FIELD

Anita Sampson, Elementary Math Coach

As a math coach, I love to think about content. When I began working with Rashelle, I was under the impression that we were launching a coaching cycle that would tackle her upcoming unit on equivalence and ordering of fractions. I was excited because this can be a challenging unit for many fourth-grade teachers, and I had lots of ideas about what it would look like now that we were using Google Classroom. Because I had heard that Rashelle was overwhelmed with the transition to teaching online, I went ahead and created some virtual lessons that she could use to get started.

During our initial conversation, Rashelle identified student engagement as her greatest area of concern. Teaching virtually was creating a situation where some students were engaged and others weren't. She explained it this way: "You know when a few students raise their hands and answer the question, and everyone else sits back and is relieved that they don't have to share? That's what's happening in the chat box during my synchronous lessons." She also shared that her team meetings would be starting soon, so she wouldn't have a lot of time to work with me. This felt like a real curveball. It became very clear that what I had planned wasn't what Rashelle needed.

I had read about mini coaching cycles as a way to work with teachers on a shorter time frame and with a narrower focus. It seemed like getting students to engage more in virtual lessons might be best tackled this way, so I suggested we do a mini coaching cycle. We spent a few co-planning and co-teaching sessions working on strategies for engaging students in online discussion. Even though it wasn't specifically math-focused, we were still using strategies that would move students toward acquisition of the content that was being taught.

I learned some key lessons through this experience. The first was a reminder to think about content and process as interconnected. It's okay to work with teachers on how to engage students in the content, especially because many of the tech tools they are using are new. Another lesson I learned is to honor the fact that right now, not every teacher is ready or has the time for coaching cycles. It felt good to work with Rashelle and her students, and I have no doubt that it will be an inroad for future coaching opportunities. I also see that I can be responsive and student-centered at the same time. I just have to remember that whatever I do as a coach, it should ultimately lead to greater student achievement. Even though we worked together for only a few sessions, I feel like I accomplished this goal.

MOVE 1: DOCUMENT THE IMPACT OF MINI COACHING CYCLES

Just as with full coaching cycles, it is critical that we document our work and the impact that it has on student and teacher learning. We do this for a number of reasons. First and foremost, we document to make sure that learning has taken place. If we are to shift the conversation from "Has it been taught?" to "Has it been learned?" then we need a way to measure student growth. When teachers see that learning has occurred, they tend to buy into the coaching process much more, and they are more likely to adopt the strategies that were used to make it happen. Second, we document for our own sense of efficacy. We both coached for years without any tangible evidence of whether or not our work was making an impact. This caused feelings of self-doubt and lack of conviction in what we were doing. As is the case with teachers, being able to see our impact creates a sense of energy and commitment to the work. Finally, we document to demonstrate the value of coaching at the district or system level. Everyone recognizes that budget cuts are likely coming as a result of the pandemic's economic fallout, so we need to be able to make the case that the investment in coaching is worth it.

In full coaching cycles, we use the Results-Based Coaching Tool (found in Resource A) as a way to document and measure teacher and student learning. However, if our intent is to move through a mini coaching cycle in just a week or two, we need something that is a bit more streamlined. Therefore, we recommend the coaching log shown in Figure 2.3. Like our other coaching logs (which are included in Resource B), it contains a series of guiding questions to steer the planning and implementation of the work. Together, these questions create a focused succession of conversations that keep student learning at the forefront. Like most of our other coaching documents, the mini coaching cycle log is meant to be shared with the partnering teacher as a way of keeping track of the work and telling the story of the partnership. This can be done through Google Docs or whatever learning management system (LMS) your school is using. The example in Figure 2.3 is from Anita's partnership with Rashelle. A blank version of this tool can be found in Resource B.

FIGURE 2.3 ● Anita and Rashelle's Mini Coaching Cycle Log

COACHING LOG: MINI COACHING CYCLE	
Teacher: Rashelle	Grade/Subject: 4th-grade math
Coach: Anita	Dates of Cycle: Sept. 11–18

1. What is the goal or target? What bigger learning does it sit under? (discussed goal on 9/11/2020)

The class is working on equivalence and ordering of fractions. Some students are having a hard time staying engaged through virtual instruction, so we are going to work on using the chat feature. The learning target is "I can use the chat feature to share my math thinking and respond to others in class discussions."

2. What evidence do we have, or need, that will inform us of where students are?

Rashelle shared that in the past few lessons, less than a handful of students had thoughtfully participated in the chat and class discussion.

3. Based on our evidence, what did we learn, and what can we try? (discussed evidence and planned on 9/16/2020)

Rashelle said that a few students were jumping in first, and then others would copy their response. There are few original responses that show what the students know. A next step is to co-teach a waterfall approach, so that the students learn how to hold their thinking and respond all at once. Math journals will also be integrated into the next lesson, so that students are doing their thinking off to the side before responding.

4. How will we co-deliver instruction? (discussed during meeting on 9/16/2020; co-taught lesson on 9/18/2020)

- Rashelle will take the lead with the lesson that will focus on how to convert negative fractions into a decimal.

COACHING LOG: MINI COACHING CYCLE

- Students will work in math journals to solve a problem and record their process. As the lesson progresses, Rashelle will introduce the waterfall approach for the chat box and will introduce the magic words: "Share your genius in 3, 2, 1." This will be done after students have done some practice and are ready to try converting a negative fraction. They will be asked to share the answer and also how they got it.

- Anita will observe the chat box, and if there are any students who respond too quickly or not at all, she'll invite them to a breakout room.

- Rashelle will lead the discussion about the thinking they shared.

- At the end of the lesson, Anita will celebrate how the students "shared their genius" in the chat box.

5. **How did the students do? What are some next steps for instruction?** (had final meeting on 9/18/2020)

More students participated in the lesson, and there was more variety in the thinking that was shared. The hope was that they'd do the work in their math journals, but there wasn't evidence that this happened. Next time, it will help to embed a timer. Rashelle also wants to have the students turn in their math journals as another form of assessment data. This will be a next step.

MOVE 2: START BY DETERMINING THE OUTCOME

Student-Centered Coaching is rooted in the belief that clarity is essential in every aspect of teaching and learning. This is certainly true in mini coaching cycles. Just as with full coaching cycles, establishing the focus for the work is the first step, because getting clear on the intended student learning is what sets us up for success in coaching, teaching, and learning.

When we determine goals for full coaching cycles, it is important that they are academic in nature and based on the standards. We use the language "Students will . . . ," and we aim for a scope that is about the length of a curricular unit. With mini coaching cycles, our focus tends to be about the size and scope of a learning target, and we often use the student-friendly language of "I can. . . ." It is also worth noting that sometimes a teacher may come to a coach with a concern that is more process- or product-oriented. If this is the case, we first strive to identify the learning that the goal sits within. Using a tool or creating a piece of work is never the goal in and of itself. We always want to know how a tool or process will help students access the learning.

The example in Anita and Rashelle's coaching log illustrates this a bit further. Rashelle's fourth-grade class was working on equivalence and ordering of fractions. Rashelle reached out to Anita because a lot of students were struggling to stay engaged during the virtual class discussions. So for the mini coaching cycle, they decided to work on this learning target: "I can use the chat feature to share my math thinking and respond to others in class discussions." The learning was still about the math standard, but the mini coaching cycle focused on a process to keep the students more engaged. If the teacher wanted to focus more directly on the math standard, the goal might have been a learning target within the broader unit, such as "I can place fractions in order on a number line." Figure 2.4 provides a comparison of goals for full and mini coaching cycles.

FIGURE 2.4 ● Comparison of Full and Mini Coaching Cycle Goals

FULL COACHING CYCLE GOALS (TAKE PLACE OVER FOUR TO SIX WEEKS)	MINI COACHING CYCLE GOALS OR TARGETS (TAKE PLACE OVER ONE TO TWO WEEKS)
• Students will write an opinion piece that uses multiple sources to justify their position.	• I can make a clear thesis statement to inform the reader of my opinion.
• Students will use a variety of strategies to solve two-digit multiplication problems in standard form and in real-world scenarios.	• I can show my thinking in my digital math journal.
• Students will identify the various ecosystems in our state and determine how they are being impacted and transformed by climate change.	• I can demonstrate my understanding in an interactive video.
• Students will identify and analyze relationships between key people and groups in the Vietnam War based on information from a variety of texts.	• I can determine at least two key people or groups in the Vietnam War from my reading.

MOVE 3: GROUND THE WORK IN DIFFERENT FORMS OF STUDENT EVIDENCE

Stages 2 and 3 of a mini coaching cycle may happen in two separate sessions, but because they are so intricately connected, they often occur within the same coaching conversation.

FIND OUT WHAT THEY ALREADY KNOW

All good instruction starts with the question "Where are the students now?" If we don't know where students are starting out as learners, what they are already bringing to the table, and what gaps or misconceptions they have, our instruction cannot be tailored to meet their needs. This can lead to wasted time, either because things are covered that the students already know or because they don't yet have all the requisite knowledge or skills to be successful in the learning. We should never waste valuable instructional time, especially now in light of all the limitations we are facing around how we can teach and engage with kids. Therefore, it is essential to start from a place of knowing where students are.

In a full coaching cycle, the teacher and coach partner to design a pre-assessment that provides valuable insights about where the students are at the beginning of the unit. Because mini coaching cycles happen on a much smaller scale, a teacher may already have some student evidence that can be used to plan next steps. Rashelle came to Anita because her students weren't engaged in the online discussions. Clearly, there was no need to collect more evidence. When the teacher does not come with evidence already in hand, the coach and teacher can determine what they will collect and analyze in order to get a sense of where the students are before planning next steps. This can often take place within the LMS and could include work that is done in platforms for collaboration, such as Google Docs, Padlet, Flipgrid, and so on. These types of coaching questions may surface what already exists: "What have you noticed so far?" or "What have you tried already, and is there any student evidence that we can use?"

USE EVIDENCE TO DRIVE INSTRUCTION

Once the teacher and coach have determined where the students are starting out as learners, they can better pinpoint the instruction that is needed to help students meet the goal or target. When co-planning the lesson, we want to think about the specific components, what will be happening in each part, and what tools or resources will be needed. We also want to consider how students will demonstrate their understanding, so that we can use that evidence for future planning. This may involve simply being intentional about whatever work they will be producing in the lesson, or it may mean that the teacher and coach discuss a specific formative assessment that is open-ended and shows what the students can understand, know, and do.

Tool: Things to Keep in Mind When Co-Planning

- ❑ Look for evidence that's easy to collect and analyze. This should be a quick process.

- ❑ Make sure the evidence is aligned with the designated outcome for learning.

- ❑ Keep an asset-based perspective. Focus on what kids already know, so that you can build from there.

- ❑ When co-planning instruction, think of what each student will need in order to be successful.

- ❑ Consider various ways in which students can demonstrate learning, especially in digital platforms.

Message From Coach Carrie

Dear Teachers,

Alright, it has happened. The questions of "Now, what exactly do you do?" "How does this coaching thing work?" and "Why are you always creeping around?" have been asked. Thankfully these questions were asked directly to me so that I can provide a response.

The short answer: I collaborate with teachers to design instruction to meet the needs of students. Below is a more detailed description of options a teacher can choose for collaboration. Spots are allocated on a first-come, first-served basis.

Option 1: Full Coaching Cycle (sign up here)

A full coaching cycle usually involves working with a teacher or a group of teachers within a whole unit. This partnership lasts four to six weeks. It includes choosing learning targets, examining student work to inform decisions, co-planning, co-teaching, and reflecting on student achievement and instructional strategies within a whole unit. During the cycle, planning meetings are held once a week, and co-teaching occurs two to three times a week. Both remote and face-to-face teachers are welcome to participate.

Option 2: Mini Coaching Cycle (sign up here)

A mini cycle is similar to a full coaching cycle but on a smaller scale. Mini cycles include choosing a learning target for focus, collecting evidence of student work related to the target, using the evidence to co-plan a lesson, co-teaching the lesson, and reflecting on whether the students met the target and planning next steps. This process usually lasts one to two weeks. During the cycle, there may be only one or two planning meetings, with co-teaching occurring on the day of the lesson. This also applies to remote and face-to-face teachers.

Option 3: In-Class Support (sign up here)
(If it is an immediate need, e-mail me.)

An instructional coach can provide support to students and teachers while instruction is occurring either in remote or face-to-face classrooms. Are you doing an activity where an extra hand would be nice? Would you like to try something new but are a little nervous about how it might go? Are you looking for some new ideas on how to help your students during class time? Would you like to observe another teacher implementing an instructional strategy but are not sure how to arrange coverage for your own class? These are times when an instructional coach can help.

Option 4: Technical Support (e-mail me)

An instructional coach can provide support with technology. If you need help with Google Classroom, Canvas, Zoom, Seesaw, Screencastify, etc., the coach can step in to help.

Unofficial Option: Sanity Support

If you need a quick breather or bathroom break, just catch me as I walk by, or e-mail me, and if I'm close by, I will try to help. If you need chocolate, stop by my office.

In Learning,

Carrie

MOVE 4: CO-TEACH THE LESSON SYNCHRONOUSLY OR ASYNCHRONOUSLY

With a lesson plan in place, it's time to think about what co-teaching will look like and how the coach will be in tune with the partnering teacher. For many of us, teaching has always happened in a silo; the only time another adult has been in our classroom is when the principal comes in to evaluate us. So the notion of co-teaching can seem foreign and even a bit threatening to some teachers. Whether working virtually or in person, we want to be explicit and intentional about the roles the teacher and coach will each play in the various parts of the lesson. This can involve virtual and in-person co-teaching moves such as Noticing and Naming, Teaching in Tandem, and Co-conferring, all of which will be explored further in Chapter 5. To help set clear expectations around each person's role in a co-taught lesson, many coaches find it helpful to use a tool like the Planner for Sharing Lessons, which is shown in Figure 2.5 (a blank copy can be found in Resource C).

FIGURE 2.5 ● Anita and Rashelle's Planner for Sharing Lessons

Learning Target: I can use the chat feature to share my math thinking and respond to others in class discussions.

WHAT'S HAPPENING? (LESSON COMPONENTS)	WHAT WILL IT LOOK LIKE?	WHO WILL TAKE THE LEAD? WHAT WILL THE OTHER "TEACHER" DO?
Lesson Opening	• Welcome students • Be sure to acknowledge each student by name • Introduce Anita • Fist to Five: How are you feeling today?	• R will welcome • A knows some Ss and will be sure to say hello • R and A will explain why A is here • A will ask how they're feeling
Review, Explore, Practice	• What do we already know? • Revisit the concept of negative value • Teach how to convert fractions to decimal	• R will lead

WHAT'S HAPPENING? (LESSON COMPONENTS)	WHAT WILL IT LOOK LIKE?	WHO WILL TAKE THE LEAD? WHAT WILL THE OTHER "TEACHER" DO?
Sharing Thinking	• Explain the waterfall approach	• R will explain • A will monitor chat and invite kids to breakout • R will lead discussion on their thinking
Wrap Up	• Share some observations about students' math thinking • Celebrate how students shared their genius	• A will lead, with R adding in

Even though Anita had documented the co-teaching plan in her coaching log, she wanted to be explicit about roles during the lesson because she and Rashelle had never worked together before. Especially with the added uncertainty of delivering lessons in a virtual format, Anita wanted to use this opportunity to build trust with Rashelle and make sure she felt completely comfortable with the process.

MOVE 5: REFLECT AND CO-PLAN THE NEXT LESSON

Because the assess–plan–teach approach is cyclical, the end of the mini coaching cycle will feel a lot like the beginning. When the lesson is finished and there is a fresh set of student evidence, it's time to plan the next lesson. This may include another round of co-teaching, or the teacher may move on alone with the planned instruction, and the cycle will draw to a close. Either way, we want to ensure that the next lesson is thoughtfully planned based on what just took place. Figure 2.6 shows a portion of the evidence from Rashelle and Anita's lesson.

In Figure 2.7, we can see how Anita and Rashelle used the evidence they collected during their co-taught lesson to sort students into groups based on how they did in relation to the learning target. A tool like the Four-Square Planner helps us

FIGURE 2.6 ● Evidence From the Co-taught Lesson

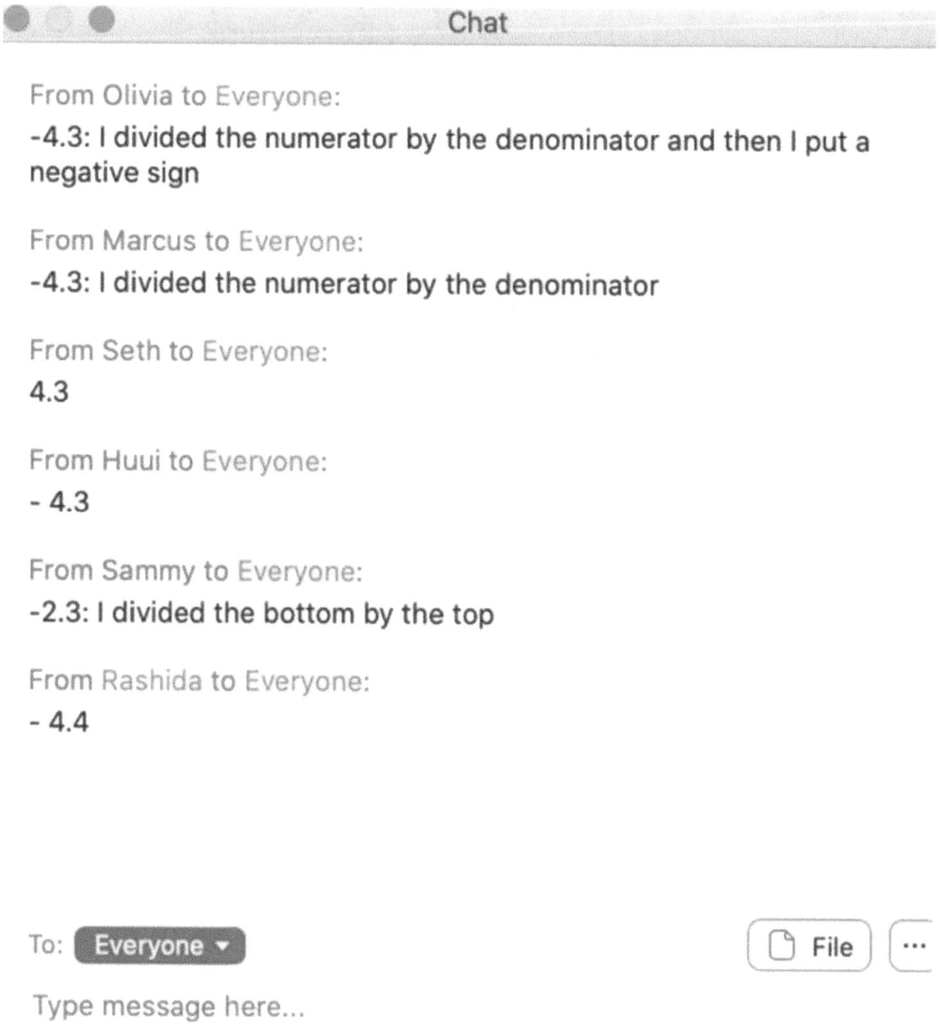

Chat

From Olivia to Everyone:
-4.3: I divided the numerator by the denominator and then I put a negative sign

From Marcus to Everyone:
-4.3: I divided the numerator by the denominator

From Seth to Everyone:
4.3

From Huui to Everyone:
- 4.3

From Sammy to Everyone:
-2.3: I divided the bottom by the top

From Rashida to Everyone:
- 4.4

To: **Everyone ▼**   [File] [···]

Type message here...

---

create targeted, relevant, and differentiated instruction. While we don't engage in a formal exit interview as we do in full coaching cycles, this move ensures that reflection on "how it went" and "what comes next" is still a key part of the process.

Sometimes this is the end of the story, and the coach moves on to work with other teachers. We've also seen many examples of a mini coaching cycle leading to more formal work with a coach. Either way, coaches can wrap up a mini coaching cycle knowing they were responsive to teachers' needs while also having a meaningful impact on student learning.

FIGURE 2.7 ● Anita and Rashelle's Four-Square Planner

FOUR-SQUARE PLANNER	
Students who shared their answer and thoroughly explained their thinking: • Cody • Marcus • Maria • Olivia • Sammy	Students who shared their answer but didn't explain how they solved the problem: • Adrienne • Huui • Jessica • Matthew • Mia • Rashida • Seth
No response: • Aditha • An Ni • Chase • Sade	Other: • Ciara was absent • Michelle had tech problems

Whole-Class Instruction

Continue practicing the waterfall approach for putting ideas in the chat. We need to focus on what elaboration looks like. Let's come up with success criteria for what a good math journal includes and teach that in a few more lessons.

MORE TIPS FOR MINI COACHING CYCLES

We'd like to point out that Rashelle and Anita's mini coaching cycle came from an authentic need that was expressed by Rashelle. This is often how a mini coaching cycle begins. If we can provide quick wins that support teachers, they will view coaching as being worth their time. Mini coaching cycles give teachers the chance to experience a taste of what it means to be coached in a student-centered manner.

Some schools have launched their coaching program with mini coaching cycles. An international school we've worked with invited all elementary teachers to participate in a mini coaching cycle when the program launched. This experience provided teachers with a clear vision for what coaching would look like in the upcoming year. When the program moved to the secondary level, the school used the same approach to build goodwill and a general understanding of coaching with this new group of teachers.

We can't say enough that mini coaching cycles don't replace full cycles. They are simply a tool that allows a coach to use student-centered practices in a shorter window of time. We feel that we must be honest that mini coaching cycles aren't measured to the same level of depth as full cycles; therefore, they won't make the same impact on student and teacher learning. That said, no contractor would ever tell you that having fewer tools is a good idea. So let's put mini coaching cycles in our toolbox, with the understanding of what they can help us accomplish as coaches.

What Can We Carry Forward?

As the landscape of how we hold school continues to provide new challenges with each passing day, everyone within the school community has had to learn and grow in order to adapt and meet the needs of students. For coaches, this has often involved being compassionate about how overwhelmed teachers may be feeling right now while also striving to keep student learning front and center in their work. While we are all ready for things to stabilize and return to some sense of pre-pandemic normalcy, we have learned much during this challenging time that we want to hold on to. Here's a list of what we hope to carry into the future:

- Coach within the assess–plan–teach process as a way to build capacity around sound instructional practice.

- Use mini coaching cycles as an option for coaching that is both student-centered and responsive to the needs of teachers.

- Use mini coaching cycles as a way to expose teachers to Student-Centered Coaching and as a catalyst for enrolling teachers into full coaching cycles.

CHAPTER 3

Use Student Evidence From a Distance

With online learning, students are producing so many pieces of work that it's overwhelming many teachers to think about how to give feedback.

—A Middle School Instructional Coach's Comment on Facebook

Now that we've had some time to settle into distance learning, we are hopefully beyond the place of addressing immediate needs of safety and access. This allows us to look more deeply into how we can actually teach our students in the best way possible under the current circumstances. By now, we are seeing fewer teachers coming to coaches with questions about technology or how to work in the learning management system (LMS). More are wondering about how to structure teaching and learning to adapt to the current circumstances. Many coaches are hearing questions like "What kinds of work should students be doing?" "How can my kids show their learning?" and "How do we give feedback in our current school setting?" In some grade levels and content areas, it feels like the students are producing mountains of work, while in others, it seems hard to imagine what that could even look like right now.

As we aim to address these questions, a few things are clear. The first is that this moment is calling on us to be innovators.

The second is that while we need to think in new ways, we also mustn't forget what we know about best instructional practice. The third is that coaches can play an important role in helping all of us rise to the occasion.

MOVE 1: THINK IN NEW WAYS ABOUT STUDENT EVIDENCE

Let's start with a reminder of what we're talking about when we refer to "student evidence" within the context of Student-Centered Coaching. As we discussed in *Student-Centered Coaching: The Moves* (Sweeney & Harris, 2017), schools today are awash in data—from district- and state-level tests, to interim assessments, to everything we use in data teams and share on data walls. In fact, in the absence of being able to collect some of this information while teaching remotely, many schools are relying on test scores from last year to plan instruction and interventions for their students. In thinking about this kind of data, we explain:

> Looking at quantitative data can be useful to identify school or district-wide trends and achievement gaps and to set big-picture goals. But when thinking about partnering with teachers through student-centered coaching, we need to use an entirely different type of data. We are looking for student evidence that we can collect *today* and that will inform us about what our students need *tomorrow*. So instead of looking at spreadsheets from big formal tests, we look at things like student writing samples, math problems, exit slips, and responses to reading. In this way, we can gain an understanding of where students are in relation to that day's learning and plan for next steps in instruction moving forward. (p. 106)

If student evidence is a driver for knowing where students are in relation to the desired learning, teachers and coaches need to be thoughtful about what kinds of evidence they use. A broad variety of digital tools is available, along with more traditional forms of student evidence, such as writing samples and exit slips (see Figure 3.1 for some examples). Because there are so many options, we thought it would be helpful to consider the qualities that make the evidence useful in propelling student learning forward. Regardless of setting, teachers and coaches will find student evidence most helpful when

- it doesn't take long to create;

- it isn't necessarily something "extra" but can be what students are already producing;

- it is descriptive in nature and makes thinking visible;

- it is aligned with desired learning outcomes, standards, and learning targets; and

- it can be produced and shared virtually.

FIGURE 3.1 ● Examples of In-Person and Virtual Student Evidence

EXAMPLES OF IN-PERSON STUDENT EVIDENCE	EXAMPLES OF VIRTUAL STUDENT EVIDENCE
Anecdotal evidence from conference notes or a Noticing and Naming Grid	Anecdotal evidence collected from notes or with a Noticing and Naming Grid in a virtual lesson
Student journals from reading, writing, math, or science	Digital reflection journals and photos of work
Quizzes or exit/entrance tickets	Online quizzes from Pear Deck, NearPod, etc.
Anything students are already producing in class	Digital work from Padlet, Flipgrid, video, etc.

BE THOUGHTFUL ABOUT THE AGE LEVEL AND CONTENT AREA

The pivot to remote learning has caused an incredible level of acceleration in the area of technology integration. For teachers who weren't accustomed to using EdTech tools, they have suddenly found themselves in a crash course on things like Canvas, Google Classroom, Padlet, Quizlet, and perhaps even Zoom. And while many educators have been successfully using these tools for some time now, it has also been exciting to see the new resources that have sprouted up in recent months. While these tools and programs offer lots of possibilities for students to demonstrate their learning, there are a few notable circumstances where we have to think even more outside the box about how to collect student evidence.

One of these areas relates to the age and developmental stage of the students we are working with. It's great to think of all the ways fourth graders to high schoolers can easily access and use technology, but what about our PreK and primary students? Jessy, an elementary coach, recently shared how she faced this issue when co-planning a writing unit with a first-grade team. When doing similar planning with the upper elementary grades in her school, they created digital writers' notebooks for students in Google Docs. This provided an easy and efficient way for students to share their writing and for the teachers and coach to give feedback through the comment feature. But what about six- and seven-year-olds, most of whom are still spelling phonetically, developing their handwriting skills, and relying heavily on pictures to help tell their story? Jessy and the team grappled with this and came up with three ideas to try. The first involved using Flipgrid, so that students could take a video of themselves reading their stories as they pointed to words. The second was having students take a "story selfie," or a picture of their story, and upload it into the LMS. The third was a "give one, get one" plan where family members could pick up a blank story packet for their student and then would receive a new one each time they brought a completed packet back to the school. In coming up with three different options, Jessy led the team in thinking about equity by providing options for people to choose which method would work best for them and their student. This also put the group squarely in the learner mindset by giving several things a try to see what would get the best results.

WHAT ABOUT ANECDOTAL EVIDENCE?

There seems to be an age-old debate in education about the value of qualitative versus quantitative data. We recognize that both are important and strongly believe that anecdotal evidence can be a valuable tool for understanding where individual students are at any given moment. It's easy to limit our view of "evidence" by solely including tangible things that students have produced or created. Yet we can also gain evidence through what we observe students doing or by what they tell us directly, as in reading and writing conferences. For coaches, anecdotal evidence is gathered in the moves for co-teaching, such as You Pick Four, Co-conferring, and Noticing and Naming. These moves, particularly what they look like when coaching from a distance, will be explored in Chapter 5.

DISPATCH FROM THE FIELD

Rachel Jenner, High School Instructional Coach

I was recently partnering with Rebekka, an instructor in the Health Careers (CNA) program at the high school technical center where I coach. Rebekka was committed to providing her students with hands-on, interactive activities during the limited time they were in the building, so we decided to record more traditional lectures for students to view prior to coming to class. This was especially important for them to earn their contact hours (as required by the State Board of Nursing). Rebekka's stress level was high because she was spending a significant amount of time preparing the videos. Yet even with all her effort, it was unclear whether students were gleaning pertinent information or even viewing the videos, and we were unable to gain a sense of their knowledge through class because only a handful of students were engaging in the discussions. As Rebekka and I reflected on the situation, we realized that we hadn't planned for how the students could demonstrate their understanding of the material. That was quite an aha for us!

The first thing we did was tackle the issue of the recorded lectures. When students got to class, we started with an open-ended entrance ticket in Google Docs. This allowed us to see what information they retained from the lecture, and it opened up a conversation about why some students might not be viewing the videos and how we could work with them to make that happen. In other words, it gave us valuable insight about where they were with both the content and the process. We then revisited their entrance tickets at the beginning of each class period, asking students to add information so that they (and we) could see their additional learning.

We also needed a way to hear from more than just a few students during class discussions. To do this, we used whiteboards to allow every student the chance to answer Rebekka's questions. I kept track of the responses to those questions so that we could use that information when we planned

(Continued)

(Continued)

the next lesson. This provided yet more evidence of student understanding and really increased classroom engagement.

The third thing we did was look at the multiple-choice tests that the students completed. We focused on what questions were discussed in station activities, discussion, or lecture; analyzed the types of questions (recall, vocabulary, analysis, etc.); and looked at trends since the beginning of the year. This helped us identify some next steps for students who didn't quite get there and some places where we might restructure the next unit to ensure all students could access the necessary information. In our reflection, Rebekka noted that it was energizing and gratifying to see multiple sources of evidence of student learning.

It's easy to focus on just the few students who answer discussion questions or a test score at the end of a unit. But using student evidence in this way gave us a really clear picture of how each student was progressing in their learning and how we could plan instruction to best meet their needs moving forward.

MOVE 2: KNOW WHAT YOU ARE LOOKING FOR

As Brené Brown likes to say, "clear is kind." Though she may be referring to leadership practices around tough conversations, this adage has proven to be true in teaching and learning as well. The main reason, which is addressed in every chapter in this book, is teacher clarity. Knowing what the intended learning is for students enables teachers and coaches to co-plan instruction that leads students down a purposeful and aligned path to the desired outcome, rather than just hoping they will eventually get there (and often wondering why they did not). Visible Learning research finds the effect size of teacher clarity to be 0.75, which is almost twice the average effect size of one year of schooling (Hattie, 2019).

Clarity also helps create the means by which all students and their caregivers understand the intended learning and what it will take to be successful in that learning. Townsley and Knight (2020) recently pointed out the heightened urgency for meaningful feedback:

With students learning independently, with caregivers, or with tutors, it is increasingly important for teachers to communicate students' strengths and weaknesses on specific skills; posting vague assignment scores leaves distance learners at a loss for how to improve and teachers wondering which learning gaps they need to fill when students return face-to-face. (para. 22)

If we expect our families to "homeschool" their students during virtual schooling, they need to know the expected outcome of any given lesson, task, or activity. These days, clarity is for them as much as it is for us.

CLARITY OF HOW THE EVIDENCE WILL BE USED

We know that part of co-planning high-quality instruction, whether remotely or in person, is thinking about how students will be able to demonstrate their understanding. In addition to determining what we will have students create, we also want to be thoughtful about *why* we are asking them to do this and *how* we will use this information. In other words, clarity of purpose is important (and kind), too.

Many of us are finding that distance learning has opened opportunities for students to produce more work than ever before. In the absence of lectures and classroom discussions, some teachers feel the need to assign some kind of "work" for students to be doing at every turn. As the coach who was quoted at the beginning of this chapter shared, the question then becomes one of how to manage giving feedback for all that work.

Coaches can be of great assistance to teachers in managing the feedback issue—but not by taking half of the virtual stack of work and doing it themselves, for this won't really help teachers in the long run. Rather, coaches can partner with teachers to gain clarity about not only the learning intentions but the purpose of the work they are having students do as well.

There are three different reasons why we might use student evidence. One reason is to make instructional decisions and plan for differentiated learning for the next lesson. This is part of the assess–plan–teach cycle that we referred to in Chapter 2 and is at the core of our work as student-centered coaches. When we are sorting student work to form groups, as will be discussed later in this chapter, there may not be a need to give individual, direct feedback to each student. This is because these issues will be addressed through either whole-group or small-group instruction.

Another reason for collecting student evidence is for summative assessment. This is what we would most commonly think of as grading. There is much discussion in the field of education around the value of giving grades, but for the purposes of our discussion, we will just acknowledge that this may be one of the purposes for which a coach and teacher collect student evidence, such as with a final assignment or end-of-unit test. As we know from the research of Dylan Wiliam (2011) and others, once grades are assigned, students internalize that information, and the learning stops. So in the instances when grades must be assigned, there is no real use in taking the time to give students descriptive feedback, because they are highly unlikely to use that information in their learning. Nor would we ground many of our coaching conversations in this type of student evidence, unless it's at the end of a coaching cycle when we want to document the overall student growth across the unit.

Finally, students may be producing work for the purpose of practice and improvement. As with any skill, they need lots of opportunity for repeated practice to gain a thorough understanding or automaticity. When students can check their own work or get feedback from a peer or teacher, they are able to learn from their mistakes as they continue to build the desired skill. Thus, if coaches and teachers have established clarity of the desired learning, they are in a better position to offer students the explicit feedback they need to move forward as learners.

Hopefully, as coaches and teachers think through the purpose of the work they're asking students to do, it will become clear that giving feedback doesn't have to feel like such an overwhelming task, even when teaching from a distance. The following list of questions can guide coaches in conversations about gaining clarity around learning and purpose.

Tool: Language for Gaining Clarity

- What is the intended learning for this unit or lesson? What standard(s) does it address?

- What will it look like if students are successful in this learning?

- How can students demonstrate their understanding, either digitally or in person?

- Is there anecdotal evidence we can collect?

- What is the purpose of the work students are creating? How will it be used?

- If students are receiving feedback, will it be descriptive or evaluative (such as a letter grade)?

MOVE 3: LOOK FOR AND BUILD ON STUDENTS' STRENGTHS

Another way coaches can support teachers in getting the most out of using student evidence is by helping them take an asset-based approach to the process. This holds true whether learning is virtual, in person, or hybrid. One way of thinking about this is as a strengths-based perspective, or focusing on what students can do and building on those strengths. But taking this approach goes beyond just acknowledging what students already know and can do. According to the California Department of Education (2020), an asset-based approach to teaching views "the diversity that students bring to the classroom, including culture, language, disability, socio-economic status, immigration status, and sexuality as characteristics that add value and strength to classrooms and communities" (para. 1).

So what does this mean for coaches? We believe in modeling an asset-based approach through our own language. When looking at student evidence with a teacher or team, we can frame the conversation around first uncovering students' schema and the skills they already have. This will lead into planning for how to celebrate and build on those strengths. This is not to say that we ignore the gaps or misconceptions in understanding; rather, we don't make students' deficits the sole focus of our work.

Taking an asset-based approach also applies to collecting anecdotal evidence during lessons. Do we listen for what students are doing or what they aren't? Do we keep our eyes trained on the learning target, or do we look beyond the teaching of the day? It can be easy to slip into a deficit mind-set in these situations, as many of us have experienced. A fourth-grade teacher and coach were co-teaching a lesson that focused on the learning target "I can repeat a powerful line to add writer's craft." All around there was evidence of the students trying to meet the learning target, and as a result, they were doing some great writing. Yet during the planning conversation, the teacher kept coming back to the students' lack of paragraphs—something that wasn't the learning target for this or any recent lesson. She was so busy noticing what wasn't there that she had a hard time seeing what was there. To respond, the coach brought the teacher back to the student evidence and asked her to narrow her focus to the learning target itself. In doing so, the teacher was able to see that students were actually attempting what they had been taught in the lesson.

We share this story because if we get stuck in the rut of looking only at what's not there, we risk missing the good stuff, and we risk our students disengaging and giving up. Bemoaning the lack of paragraphs made the teacher feel hopeless. Seeing that her lesson inspired the students to try something new made her feel just the opposite.

Tool: Language for Staying Asset-Based When Looking at Student Evidence

IF I HEAR OR NOTICE . . .	THEN I CAN SAY OR DO . . .
A teacher says, "I don't know what kind of math these kids learned in their home country, but they sure don't get the way we do it here."	You can respond, "It's so fascinating that sometimes different approaches and strategies are taught in different countries. I wonder if we could ask them to show their approach in a Flipgrid to the rest of the class. That would give us insight into what they already know, and it might give the other kids some new ways of approaching the problem. It would also give these newcomers a great way to shine."
When looking at student work, a teacher complains that a student doesn't know "anything" about the concept that's being taught.	You can remind the teacher that all kids come to school with a variety of schema and that part of our job is to uncover what they already know and to build on their strengths.
A teacher says, "I just get depressed looking at my students' work because it's a reminder of how far behind they are and how much ground I have to try to make up with them."	You might say, "Even though many students in your class are below grade level, it will be helpful to figure out what each one is bringing to the learning. That way, we can address the specific things they each need, which will help accelerate their learning."

Message From Coach Carrie

Dear Teachers,

Coaching is for *everyone*. Coaching is not about "fixing" teachers.

We are all a part of a team working together for the benefit of our students. A common misconception about coaching is that it's only for teachers who need some extra

(Continued)

(Continued)

help or teachers who have been identified by administration as low-performing. This is simply not true! Think about athletic teams, debate teams, academic teams, any group where people have a coach or sponsor. The coaches and sponsors do not work with just the people who need extra help. The star of the team and the benchwarmer both receive support from a coach. Everyone works together to reach their common goal. Student-Centered Coaching is the same. Coaching focuses on a student achievement goal, and all teachers have students.

Bottom line: Student-Centered Coaching involves student-centered goals. We all have students, so coaching is for all. Reach out today!

In Learning,

Carrie

MOVE 4: SORT EVIDENCE TO DIFFERENTIATE INSTRUCTION ACROSS PLATFORMS

Using student evidence to plan instruction is a high-leverage practice. We believe that coaches have a tremendous opportunity to demonstrate the power of this practice when they partner with teachers. We sort student work with teachers because it is a productive way to help them see—and act on—the different needs of students in their classroom.

This practice is no different when coaching from a distance. What's different is the type of student evidence we use and how we sort it. Typically, a teacher or team of teachers sits down with the coach and a pile of student work and sorts that work against the learning target or success criteria. When coaching virtually, teachers and coaches find themselves analyzing evidence such as videos or work that is submitted on Seesaw, Jamboard, Padlet, Flipgrid, or Google Docs. While they may not be able to be together in person, they can still have this conversation while meeting virtually, with both people looking at the digital data at the same time. Regardless of the platform, efficiency in the process is key. Teachers have precious little planning time as it is, so we can't expect to spend an entire planning period analyzing student evidence. This part of the process should only take about ten to fifteen minutes of the allotted time, so that the rest of the planning period can be spent co-planning the lesson based on what was learned through sorting. The following protocol offers a guide for how to sort student work when coaching from a distance.

TOOL: PROTOCOL FOR SORTING STUDENT WORK FROM A DISTANCE

Purpose: To analyze student evidence in order to plan for differentiated instruction.

Suggested time: 10–15 minutes

Process:

1. Be sure that both the coach and the teacher(s) have access to the set of work. It can be housed in the LMS or in a shared document. If working in person but still at a distance, it may make sense to create a copy of the set for each person.

2. Read through the entire set of class work, looking for trends relative to the learning target(s).

3. Discuss the trends that were noticed. Collectively, decide which ones are the most significant and need further instruction—either in whole or small groups.

4. Go back to the work to sort students according to the identified needs. If something pertains to the whole class, this will be addressed in whole-group instruction.

5. Plan for instruction based on the needs of each group.

SORTING STUDENT WORK WITH GROUPS

Either through data teams or professional learning communities (PLCs), most educators have some experience with analyzing student data as a group. When coaching teams, we find this practice to be most meaningful when the group examines a single class set of work and then uses the trends identified in the process to analyze and sort the evidence from their own class. Approaching the process this way increases efficiency because only one class set is being sorted, and it gives the "presenting" teacher the opportunity to have a fresh set of eyes on their students. When coaching from a distance, this is still a powerful shared learning experience, with the coach leading a virtual conversation among two to four teachers about a single collection of digital student work that they can all access.

There may be cases in which the group of teachers prefers to spend their time analyzing their own set of class work. When this is the case, we recommend that sorting take place prior to the group coming together to meet virtually. This assumes, of course, that teachers are comparing against clear success criteria to ensure that everyone is looking at their work through the same lens. Once group members have sorted their own evidence, the group can convene to co-plan instruction based on the common trends they found in the work.

CREATE AN OPPORTUNITY FOR FEEDBACK

Most of us have typically received feedback as an event, when someone observes us doing something and then sits us down and tells us what they think. This is likely the way we are used to giving feedback as well, including in our coaching. With Student-Centered Coaching, however, we believe that feedback happens in a partnership between the coach and the teacher. It is not something that one party gives to the other; rather, it is co-constructed throughout the various steps of the coaching cycle. We refer to this as Strengths-Based Feedback, and it has three steps:

1. **Clarify** to understand the whole picture.
2. **Value** what is already working.
3. **Uncover possibilities** for what might come next.

Engaging in sorting sessions with teachers in any setting creates rich opportunities for this kind of reflective feedback to take place. This is because when we look at evidence with the intention of understanding how each student progressed in relation to the intended learning, it naturally leads us to consider *why* students fared the way they did. After a lesson, we might typically expect a coach to tell a teacher something like this: "I think that lesson went pretty well for most kids because the part you modeled was really explicit. You lost some of them in the guided practice, so be sure to break down the steps more clearly next time." Imagine instead how much more meaningful and less threatening it would be for the coach and teacher to ask themselves questions such as these:

- Overall, how do we feel the lesson went based on how the students did?

- What are some specific things that helped the students meet the target?

- What can we try differently next time?

Engaging in this kind of Strengths-Based Feedback ensures that the analysis of student evidence will result in a positive learning experience for students—and for teachers as well.

What Can We Carry Forward?

Sorting student evidence is a practice that's rooted in formative assessment and is a key driver in Student-Centered Coaching. Whether coaching in person or at a distance, our hope is that coaches will continue to pursue partnerships with teachers that leverage this important instructional practice. As we push into new frontiers with distance learning and coaching, here are a few things we hope will carry forward into the future:

- Continue to use high-quality EdTech tools for students to demonstrate their understanding.

- Increase the emphasis on clarity for teachers, students, and caregivers.

- Make an ongoing commitment to maintaining an asset-based perspective with students.

- Maintain a flexible mindset about what qualifies as student evidence.

CHAPTER 4

Co-Plan With Teachers and Teams

When instructional design moves online and student submissions follow, we fast-forward to a transparent and objective body of student work. This work, intimately tied to instructional design, can now more than ever be leveraged for Student-Centered Coaching.

—Sean Nash, District Coordinator of Science, North Kansas City School District

It's fair to say that by now, most districts have a learning management system (LMS) to house and organize instructional materials. Some are adopting an LMS for the first time, and others have already been one-to-one (one device per student) for a while. How we adapt to these new technologies is presenting unexpected opportunities for coaching. This doesn't mean that coaches become all things tech support. What it does mean is that they can now tuck their coaching work into an LMS, adding a level of coherence and structure that never existed before.

When we started as teachers, our lessons were written in oversized spiral notebooks with the days of the week across the top and the time blocks down the side. Our biggest innovation was using different colored ink or sticky notes to code our lessons. It almost seems quaint to think about that in an era when almost every document we create can be directly shared with others. Teachers are now able to plan collaboratively, and coaches can join right in to ensure that teachers or teams are able to design instruction that is engaging, rigorous, and integrates technology. The moves that are provided in this chapter will help coaches make the most out of the virtual and in-person planning opportunities that they have with teachers and teams.

MOVE 1: LEVERAGE AND EMBRACE TECHNOLOGY

Never having been EdTech gurus ourselves, we'd hear stories about how the future was in blended learning or flipped classrooms. We agreed that it seemed compelling, but it also seemed like a long way off. Little did we know that we'd all be there much quicker than expected.

Blended learning used to be considered innovative and outside the box. It was most frequently found in schools that were lucky enough to have the resources that are needed to adopt one-to-one programs. When the pandemic hit in March 2020, these schools were able to make the transition to remote teaching more easily. For schools without this level of tech integration, the transition has been much more challenging. This revealed the inequalities in our school systems. While they've always been there, the shift to virtual learning has made them ever more apparent. The role coaches have played during this time has varied based on how long these programs have been in place. Some coaches easily transitioned to coaching online because the teachers already had the systems in place for blended learning. Others have been supporting teachers in learning how to use a new LMS, helping students navigate issues such as Wi-Fi and computer access, and other duties that might fall outside of a typical coach's role.

TECHNOLOGY CAN OPEN DOORS

Some years back, Diane was a literacy coach in four elementary schools in northeast Denver. Much of her time involved driving from school to school to attend meetings with teachers and principals. Just think how much more efficient she would have been if some of these meetings had been held online. We recognize that meeting virtually will never replace spending time in classrooms, but we can't deny these efficiencies.

Coaches are finding that technology can open doors for collaboration with teachers. Scheduling time together has always been a challenge because teachers are so busy throughout the school day. Now that we can use applications like Zoom, Google Meet, or Microsoft Teams, we are able to stay more connected. Another factor is the cultural shift of working from home. This is something that we never could have imagined would happen among the teaching ranks, yet it did. Today, Zooming into a person's living room is no longer awkward or off limits, even when dogs and babies pay us a visit.

We admit that none of this is perfect, and we have all experienced Zoom fatigue. Liz Fosslien and Mollie West Duffy from the *Harvard Business Review* (2020) explain it this way:

> Zoom fatigue stems from how we process information over video. On a video call the only way to show we're paying attention is to look at the camera. But, in real life, how often do you stand within three feet of a colleague and stare at their face? Probably never. This is because having to engage in a "constant gaze" makes us uncomfortable—and tired. (para. 5)

The following tool provides strategies for maintaining a healthy mindset, so that our online planning sessions can be as productive as possible.

Source: istock.com/wsfurlan

Tool: Strategies for Being Productive in Tech-Based Co-Planning Sessions

❏ Mix standing and sitting during co-planning sessions.

❏ Tell the teacher(s) that you may not focus on the camera because you will be capturing the conversation in a coaching log.

❏ Avoid multitasking.

❏ Turn off onscreen notifications.

❏ Hide "self-view" so that you don't watch yourself.

❏ Always schedule movement breaks between calls.

❏ Stay hydrated, and don't forget the snacks!

MOVE 2: START FROM THE INTENDED LEARNING

When we initially moved to remote learning, many teachers spent their time creating lessons to keep students busy and engaged. For schools without an LMS, this took the form of packets of lessons and activities. For one-to-one schools, teachers posted lessons online that they hoped would keep the students involved as they adjusted to this new way of doing school. The velocity of the change meant that teachers didn't have a whole lot of time to step back and think about coherence in the lessons they were putting together. With more time under our belt, districts are circling back to the important practice of clearly identifying the intended learning, and that sits within the curriculum.

We know that the first step for planning always begins with the intended learning. This is because it increases teacher clarity, which in turn helps students understand what is expected. O'Connell and Vandas (2015) write:

> Clarity around understanding the standards and what must be learned and taught begins with the

teacher. It is absolutely imperative that the teacher find clarity in the standards in order to translate clear learning expectations for students. If the teacher is unclear about what students must know and be able to do, it is impossible for students to follow or own their learning. (p. 54)

Figuring out what we want the students to know and be able to do means we must push ourselves beyond what's on the test to thinking about learning in the truest sense of the word.

This isn't always as straightforward as it sounds. Take this experience from Sienna, a middle school ELA coach. In a planning conversation with a team that was about to begin a writing unit, Sienna thought they would first discuss the intended learning. What happened instead is that the teachers jumped right to sharing lessons that they had taught in the past. While Sienna wanted to honor their ideas, she also knew that they shouldn't go straight to lessons and activities before they had established clarity around the bigger ideas of the unit. It was uncomfortable to redirect the group and ask them to slow down, but she took this step because she knew that now was the time to do this important work.

On further reflection, Sienna realized that she opened the door for this by starting the meeting with this message: "Let's talk about how we want to tackle this unit." Instead, she could have said, "Let's start by framing the intended learning, and then we can discuss the lessons that we will teach." If she had been explicit from the start, it would have been an easier and more efficient meeting. This is something that matters today more than ever. In this example, the meeting was in person, but we know that with so many of these conversations taking place from a distance, it is even more important to have a clear process or protocol that sets us on the right course. The following tools provide a protocol for co-planning units, as well as language for when these meetings get tricky.

TOOL: PROTOCOL FOR CO-PLANNING UNITS

1. Determine the goal or intended learning for the unit. Just like a coaching cycle goal, this can be framed as "Students will...."

2. Unpack the learning intention into a set of learning targets ("I can..." statements). These targets will serve as the success criteria.

3. Plan the classwork, texts, and resources that will be needed to address each learning intention.

4. Plan how the learning intentions and/or learning targets will be assessed.

Tool: Language for Keeping Planning Conversations Focused on Learning

IF I HEAR OR NOTICE...	THEN I CAN SAY OR DO...
When engaged in planning conversations, teachers immediately share activities that they found online.	Begin by thanking the teachers for researching and sharing their lesson ideas. Then nudge the conversation by saying, "What if we create a list of the learning targets? Then we can come up with some ideas for lessons. This way we'll be sure we are aligned with the standard."
Teachers aren't on the same page with their units. This is creating variations in the level of rigor that students are experiencing from classroom to classroom.	Meet with the principal to determine how to pull teachers together to do some unit planning. It would be up to the principal to frame why this is important and what the expectations are for teachers.
Sometimes it's hard to keep up in coaching conversations, and it feels embarrassing to ask someone to repeat themselves. This is especially hard when meetings are online.	Use a protocol for lesson and unit planning. This will provide a structure for the planning conversations. This can be as simple as a series of questions to guide you through the process.

HOW DO LEARNING INTENTIONS AND LEARNING TARGETS FIT TOGETHER?

You may be wondering how learning intentions and learning targets relate to one another. A learning intention is the broader intended learning. It may begin with the words "I am learning . . ." or "Students will . . ." (for example, "I am learning how to read and learn from informational text"). Learning intentions often become our goals for a coaching cycle because they are broad in scope, are open-ended, and require multiple lessons and learning experiences for students to get there.

A learning target on other hand, sits beneath the learning intention. A collection of learning targets makes up success criteria that are used throughout any given unit. An example of a learning target would be "I can stop and jot when I encounter something in the text that I didn't already know" or "I can keep track of new vocabulary as I read." These are just some examples of learning targets that serve to define what learning looks like underneath the broader learning intention. Both are essential elements of co-planning units and lessons.

In the book *Where Great Teaching Begins*, Anne Reeves (2011) offers a helpful way to check the quality of learning targets. She suggests that we ask whether the target "is student-centered, is thinking-centered, and describes a performance that demonstrates learning" (p. 70). When learning targets are student-centered, they focus on how students will demonstrate their new learning. When they are thinking-centered, they challenge students to expand and synthesize in relation to the content. We must continually ask whether the targets we are using paint a clear picture of our vision for student performance.

MOVE 3: CO-PLAN UNITS WITHIN THE LMS

As we mentioned earlier, crafting high-quality learning targets is an essential part of unit planning. Unfortunately, learning targets can often be misused. Instead of being a thoughtful guide for building clarity, they have been reduced to being posted on the board or in an online lesson as an objective that students pay little attention to. We can do so much more when we embed the targets into our units in a way that directly affects how our students approach their learning.

PUTTING ON OUR STUDENT HAT

When it comes to curriculum design, it can be easy to forget that our students are our customers. As educators, we so often jump right to "teacher speak" and make things far more complicated than they need to be. Designing student-facing materials means we must ensure that they are so clear that not a single student will be confused by what they are supposed to be learning and doing, and how they should be responding. This includes students who speak a language other than English, those with learning differences, and everyone else.

We can achieve this by putting on our student hat to assess whether the tasks, instructions, resources, and clickability are logical and easy to follow. Jennifer Gonzalez (2015) refers to this as "dogfooding":

> It's a term that's been used for years among software developers, and it refers to the act of using your own product *as a consumer* in order to work out its glitches, the metaphorical equivalent of "eating your own dog food." . . . For many companies, dogfooding is just part of their best practices, a natural step in software development before a product is launched for consumer use. (para. 1–2)

This is a practice that isn't limited to designing apps. It can also be applied to designing curricular units.

There are several ways in which we can partner with teachers to put on our student hat:

- Swap and read units that have been designed by someone else.

- Work the problems or tasks. See if you can get through what is assigned without asking for help.

- Imagine you are a second-language learner. Are there enough ways to navigate without a full understanding of the language? If not, how will additional support be provided?

- Are tech tips provided, such as screencasts of where to click?

WAYFINDING

Systems for navigation are essential when it comes to planning online units of study. Not everyone has a parent or guardian who can assist their student. Many of our families speak languages other than English, and one in four students has been diagnosed with dyslexia. For some students, their only experience with technology has been using a cell phone. Navigating (or failing to navigate) a unit only increases the chronic stress our students are experiencing and could be a deal breaker for some of them. This, in our opinion, is far from equitable.

In a typical classroom environment, a teacher can "read the room" and attend to students who seem confused. Hands shoot up, or one student whispers to another, "What are we supposed to do?" When we are dispersed in a remote learning environment, these cues no longer exist. As a result, students may persist in their confusion for far too long. This is especially true for second-language learners or those with learning differences. Our work rests in helping teachers build explicit cues into their lessons, so that the students can successfully move through their learning. Coaches can partner with teachers to do this through wayfinding.

Wayfinding is a term originally coined by architects in reference to airport design. Think about it—when you travel through an airport, you navigate from the curb to your gate without much more than a second thought. In the article "How You Know Where You're Going When You're in an Airport," Zweig (2014) writes that wayfinding "is the process of designing cues—from signage to lighting and color, even the architecture, anything at all—to help people navigate a built environment" (para. 7).

We can build wayfinding cues into our lessons through the use of icons, color, and a predictable and repeated structure. We can test our wayfinding cues by looking through a unit using the following guiding questions. This is a perfect role for coaches as they support teachers in developing curriculum that reaches the intended goal.

Tool: Checklist for Wayfinding

❑ How easily can the students navigate the unit?

❑ Is the format of the unit consistent?

❑ Are the icons consistent from class to class and across the school and district?

❑ Is there a logical flow and structure to the lessons?

❑ Does the ease of navigation take students into deep learning?

❑ Do any of the lessons need to be tested or practiced?

❑ Can we use colors or images to support students?

ICONS FOR WAYFINDING

The icons shown in the following tool and Figure 4.1 were originally created by Sean Nash and Sarah Christus of North Kansas City Schools. They are now used universally across content areas in grades K–12 in the district. They were built as a set of design signposts to make the navigation of learning tasks so simple for students and staff that the complexity of any form of digital learning "gets out of the way" of the actual student thinking and feedback we wish to see. Thus, it is important to use the icons in a similar way across the organization, as has been done in North Kansas City Schools.

TOOL: EXAMPLES OF WAYFINDING ICONS

 The *Think* icon. Indicates that the focus for thinking on this task follows soon after.

 The *Read* icon. Indicates the focus for reading an upcoming body of text.

 The *Write* icon. Indicates the process and content to be used in a formal or informal written response.

 The *Reflect* icon. Indicates the direct purpose for student reflection soon follows.

 The *Video* icon. Indicates video content. The purpose for listening should follow. Especially important for a video that cannot be embedded.

 The *Listen* icon. Indicates audio content. The purpose for listening should follow.

 The *Create* icon. Indicates a task that requires an original student creation beyond a text response.

 The *Design* icon. Indicates a task that requires students to craft an original design process.

 The *Solve* icon. Indicates a problem or challenge to be solved.

 The *Attention!* icon. Should be used sparingly. Indicates an instruction that, if not followed, will not allow the task to work.

Source: Created by Sean Nash and Sarah Christus. Used with permission

The examples of lessons in Figure 4.1 illustrate what it looks like to provide students with a road map for their learning, as well as clear use of icons and other cues for them to be able to navigate the work independently.

FIGURE 4.1 ● Lessons From a Sixth-Grade Science Module

ENGAGE 1—TP2—NATURAL RESOURCES

Source: istock.com/dem10

In the following series of lessons, we will explore some of Earth's most important natural resources. We will learn what these resources are, where and how they are found, and the impacts humans have on them.

But first: Let's find out what you already think/know about natural resources!

 to engage in our first exploration....

ENGAGE 2—TP2—HOW MUCH WATER IS ON EARTH, AND IS IT EVENLY DISTRIBUTED?

Source: istock.com/janrysavy

Let's begin simply by thinking about water on planet Earth. Water is certainly one of our most important natural resources. We do not know of any form of life that can exist without at least some access to water.

1. **Based on your prior knowledge and experiences . . . how much water is on Earth?** That may be tough to describe in numbers, but do the best you can. How much water is found on our planet, and

2. **Is the water found on Earth evenly distributed?** Tell whether or not you believe it is, and describe a little of what makes you say so.

REPLY below to enter your current thinking about the amount and distribution of water, and be sure to click "Post Reply" when you finish your thoughts. You may wish to check the "Show Rubric" link to the upper right to be sure your response is complete. After you post your initial thinking, please read the responses by your classmates, and consider adding some feedback to their thinking by clicking "Reply" to one or more of their responses. When you are finished for now,

click NEXT at the bottom right of the screen to enter our next exploration. . . .

EXPLAIN 1—TP2—WATER RESOURCES: WHAT CAN WE NOW EXPLAIN?

Source: Photo by Simone Bosotti. https://creativecommons.org/licenses/by-sa/2.0/

 The standards in this unit require you to be able to explain both **how and why water is distributed unevenly** on Earth and to be able to understand **how humans have an impact on water** resources.

The above is essentially a claim. It is now your job to provide evidence and reasoning to back up this claim. Think back to what you might have already known about water before this unit and what you have learned as a result of the previous tasks here.

(Continued)

FIGURE 4.1 ● (Continued)

W Simply provide evidence and reasoning in writing to back up the statement that Earth's water resources are both unevenly distributed and impacted by humans. Be sure to reference as many specific items of evidence as you can recall. Consult the rubric to make sure you are providing as much detail as possible. Your response will be seen this time only by your teacher.

---

hit REPLY below to enter your thinking about the questions posed above and be sure to click "Submit Assignment" in the upper right when you have completed your response. Use the rubric below as a tool to help you craft a complete response. The most important thing here is to provide as much detailed evidence and the reasoning behind it, in order to support the claim above.

When you have finished submitting, **click NEXT** at the bottom right of the screen to enter our next exploration....

Source: Created by Sean Nash and Sarah Christus. Used with permission.

DISPATCH FROM THE FIELD

Nicole Zito, Instructional Coach

My work as a learning coach at Nido de Aguilas in Santiago, Chile, has included partnering with my fellow coaches and teachers to uncover best practices for designing online units of study. Because we've been off campus for the past several months, this work has occurred through a combination of professional development and in one-on-one or small-group settings during established office hours. For example, I worked with another member of the coaching team to develop an opt-in workshop for secondary teachers on how to craft units that were easy to navigate, clear, and compelling for our students.

We designed an iterative experience in which teachers would empathize with their students by thinking through what they needed as learners. We started with the guiding question "What makes an online assignment easy or hard to follow for students?" Then we shared a Padlet that defined the strategy known as wayfinding and asked the teachers to write in the chat box about how navigating an airport is made easier with navigation cues. Then we discussed how airport wayfinding relates to students in distance learning. On the Padlet were images of airport cues, such as lights and signage, to inspire them.

After that, we took a few minutes to reflect on a portion of learning from a ninth-grade science unit from another teacher. We pictured ourselves as ninth graders and reflected on what we liked and what we found challenging to navigate from the posted learning tasks. After about five minutes of writing down their thoughts, we worked in breakout rooms to discuss their ideas in smaller groups. One person from each group recorded their thinking on the Padlet so that we could identify themes. When we came back together, a representative from each group shared their thinking. Together, we landed on the following strategies as being necessary for designing units that are easy for our students to navigate:

- Include the **suggested time** for each task to help students conceptualize how to pace themselves for each aspect of the assignment.

- Have **small icons** next to the tasks that depict the nature of the work, such as a book for a reading task or a lightbulb for a brainstorming task.

- The design of the page matters. **Enlarging, highlighting, italicizing and/or bolding words** emphasizes what is important. A clean page looks better.

- When the flow of learning says to **stop and check in** with a teacher before continuing, this provides the opportunity for teachers to ensure that students have feedback at critical points.

- A mix of verbal directions, perhaps as **short screencasts or recorded tutorials**, humanizes the learning.

- Working documents in which **students document their goal, reflection, and progress** could be hyperlinked to show students' process, and teachers can easily step in when students need additional support.

At the end of the workshop, the teachers went to work applying what they had discovered for an upcoming learning task. This included spending the last twenty minutes tuning into their own students' wayfinding experience. We encouraged them to continue the conversation, either in our coaching office hours or on the Padlet. This workshop was a first step in helping teachers gain new perspectives, practical suggestions for designing online learning, some technology strategies, and, most of all, greater empathy for their learners.

Message From Coach Carrie

Dear Teachers,

Thank you for welcoming me into your planning periods and classrooms these past weeks. I know times are crazy right now, so I just wanted to remind you of the support

(Continued)

(Continued)

I can provide. Attached is a link to a Google Doc listing all the options for a coaching partnership. If you are interested, click the link in the Google Doc to sign up or e-mail me. The Google Doc I mentioned is a file with the coaching options that I sent a few weeks ago.

Thank you for all that you do! I look forward to partnering with you in the near future.

In Learning,

Carrie

MOVE 4: CO-PLAN LESSONS THAT DON'T LEAVE ANY STUDENTS BEHIND

As we've discussed, co-planning lessons can occur at a distance or when we are sitting side by side with teachers. Either way, we recommend a well-articulated process that moves teachers from thinking about the target, to thinking about what each part of the lesson will look like, to planning wayfinding cues in digital lessons, to mapping out how students will be grouped and assessed.

We anticipate that teachers will be moving between virtual, hybrid, and in-person lessons for longer than any of us would like to admit. We also expect many of these practices to persist into the future. For this reason, it's helpful to keep in mind that the co-planning is what matters; where we are sitting is less important.

PLANNING FOR ALL (AND FOR A FEW)

Student-Centered Coaching is a model that is best applied to a whole class, rather than with a few select students. We worry that if we narrow our focus to just a couple of students, we may miss or lower our expectations for others. Our belief is that all students can and will meet the goals that are set. Crafting and executing the scaffolds that students need to get there is what makes coaching so valuable.

Doing this work may seem like an intense or intimidating proposition, but it doesn't have to be. We can advocate for students with evidence of their prior learning, a quality learning target, and a few carefully selected coaching questions that surface what they need to keep moving forward. This then creates the conditions for differentiated instruction that may include whole-group, small-group, or one-on-one opportunities for learning. The following tool provides coaching language for supporting teachers in planning for all students and differentiating based on their needs.

Tool: Language for Co-Planning

- What needs to be in place so that every student can be successful in this lesson?
- Do we anticipate any misconceptions among students? If so, how will they be addressed?
- In what aspects of the lesson should scaffolds be added?
- In what aspects of the lesson should scaffolds be removed?
- How will we support language development?
- How will students demonstrate understanding?
- What student evidence can we use for the next planning session?

WHEN CAN I FIND TIME TO CO-PLAN WITH TEACHERS?

We are all sensitive to the extraordinary workload that teachers are carrying right now. This has led some coaches to back off to give teachers space. The downside of this approach is that it withholds coaching support from those who might really want it. In other words, let's not make the assumption that teachers are too busy for coaching. Instead, we can offer teachers any or all of the following options. Providing teachers with these choices will engage them in a way that is flexible and responsive.

We can

- co-plan a lesson or two,
- co-plan a unit,
- co-plan within a mini coaching cycle, or
- co-plan within a full coaching cycle.

These options also provide teachers with choice regarding how much time they would like to dedicate to coaching. It puts them in the driver's seat and discourages a coach from making the assumption that everyone is too busy for coaching. You'd be amazed by the stories we are hearing about teachers who have never reached out in the past and are now requesting help and looking to partner with a coach. We know that this is a bit of a departure from our stance that most of a coach's work should be in cycles, but it very much aligns with our belief that we have to honor where teachers are in the here and now.

If we keep co-planning efficient and straightforward, teachers will see the value it brings to their work with students. The following tool is a protocol that can be used with individuals or teams. As always, we welcome you to use this as a starting point and adjust it as needed.

TOOL: PROTOCOL FOR CO-PLANNING LESSONS

1. Analyze the student work that came from previous instruction.
2. Based on the evidence, identify the learning target that will be focused on.
3. Determine what will happen synchronously and asynchronously.
4. Plan each lesson component.
5. Plan how students will show what they know. This includes how students will self-assess and how the teacher will formatively assess.
6. Determine how the students will be grouped for learning.
7. Practice the problems and tasks before teaching the lesson.

What Can We Carry Forward?

Co-planning is one of the most valuable practices we have in our tool-box. If done well, it offers immediate relief to teachers, because it provides them with someone to think through their lessons or units before they are used with students. In years past, we've heard many stories from coaches who spent time unpacking units with teachers or teams before starting a round of coaching cycles. This provided a strong curricular footing from which to coach. Today, this approach is even more important, because teachers are innovating not only how they teach but what they teach as well. When it comes to co-planning, here's what we hope to carry forward:

- Learning intentions and targets are more important than ever. This will continue well past the pandemic.

- Planning and unpacking units is a great strategy to use with teachers or teams.

- Wayfinding is an essential component of using an LMS.

- Not every planning conversation has to be within a full coaching cycle.

- Teachers value having a thinking partner when co-planning lessons.

CHAPTER 5

Co-Teach Virtually and in Person

*When I get the chance to co-teach, I really feel like
I'm a part of the classroom community.*

—Eliza Sampson, Math Coach

Entering the classrooms of other teachers can be intimidating. This may be the case for coaches if they feel unqualified because they haven't taught that grade level or subject before. It is especially true for teachers if coaching is perceived as being an evaluative process. If we are thoughtful about how we approach co-teaching in virtual and in-person classrooms, we can avoid these negative perceptions. We like to think of co-teaching as a practice that grounds our coaching in the real work of students. The classroom is where the action is, and with so many teachers trying to get a clearer sense of how their students are progressing, joining synchronous or asynchronous lessons is an important place for Student-Centered Coaching to come to life.

In *The Essential Guide for Student-Centered Coaching* (Sweeney & Harris, 2020), we define co-teaching in this way: "Rather than modeling or observing, we advocate for coaches and teachers to build partnerships while working together in the classroom. This includes using a variety of coaching moves that increase teacher metacognition and transfer of practice" (p. 11). When it comes to co-teaching, some coaching models emphasize modeling and observation as foundational practices—for example, using earbuds to cue teachers as they make specific instructional moves. Also common are video-based coaching sessions, where teachers are filmed and then analyze their practice with a coach by their side, or the practice of the coach modeling lessons as a first step to working in a classroom.

If we limit co-teaching to being only about modeling and observation, coaching may be interpreted as being judgmental or evaluative. Who hasn't felt judged when being recorded delivering a lesson? And who didn't feel undervalued when a coach assumed that you needed to see them model something before you could do it yourself? While we aren't necessarily against these practices, we do see them as only a small part of the bigger picture of what a coach can do when in another teacher's virtual or in-person classroom. We define these approaches to co-teaching as teacher-centered because the focus of the conversation is on what the teacher is or is not doing. We make this distinction because if modeling and observing are how you define co-teaching, this chapter may serve to redefine what it means to co-teach.

MOVE 1: EXPAND OUR VIEW OF CO-TEACHING

When writing our previous books, we struggled with how to name the practice that we refer to as "co-teaching." We considered "coaching in the classroom," but this didn't capture the sense of partnership we were going for. It felt more like a behavior than a way of being. Because we value the "co-," or partnership, of "co-teaching," we decided to settle there.

As we explore co-teaching throughout this chapter, we will share a series of coaching moves that fall into two categories: (1) the coach as co-assessor and (2) the coach as co-deliverer. Think of these moves as part of a flexible process that can take place during full or mini coaching cycles.

The following tool introduces how our co-teaching moves can be used across virtual and in-person settings. We have defined these moves as co-assessing and co-delivering; we will provide more detail about each of them later in this chapter.

TOOL: VIRTUAL AND IN-PERSON CO-TEACHING MOVES

MOVES FOR CO-ASSESSING		
	WHAT IT LOOKS LIKE IN A CLASSROOM	**WHAT IT LOOKS LIKE VIRTUALLY**
Noticing and Naming	During the lesson, the teacher and coach focus on how the students are demonstrating their current understanding in relation to the learning targets. As they work with students, they will record student evidence that they will use either in the moment or in future planning conversations.	The coach joins the lesson by being added to the class roster. Before the lesson, the teacher and coach plan what the students will learn, create, and do. Then they collect student evidence through a platform such as Padlet, student response, or a Google survey, or simply by listening to and recording observations from student discussions. The evidence that is collected is then used to co-plan future lessons using either a planning template or video conferencing.
You Pick Four	The teacher identifies four students whom the coach will pay special attention to during the lesson. The coach keeps the learning targets in mind while collecting student evidence. This evidence is then used in future planning conversations.	The coach and teacher choose a few students to closely monitor and assess. This leads to a conversation about how to address the needs of these students. It may also indicate when to reteach or adjust next steps.
Co-conferring	The teacher and coach sit side by side when conferring with students. This way, they create a shared understanding of how individual students are doing in relation to the learning target. This then informs the next lesson or even a reteach in the moment.	The teacher and coach schedule online check-ins, or conferences, with students. These can include discussions about acquisition of content, social-emotional check-ins, goal setting by students, or extra support.

(Continued)

(Continued)

MOVES FOR CO-DELIVERING		
Thinking Aloud	The teacher and coach share their thinking throughout the delivery of a lesson. By being metacognitive in this way, they are able to name successes and work through challenges in real time.	The teacher and coach decide how this will be accomplished based on the lesson delivery. For example, during synchronous learning, they can use the chat box to reflect on how the students are engaging. Or when learning is asynchronous, they can review student responses and discuss how they are matching the learning targets/ success criteria.
Teaching in Tandem	The teacher and coach work together to co-deliver the lesson. The lesson is co-planned to ensure that the roles are clear, that the learning targets are defined, and that the teacher and coach both understand how the lesson is crafted.	The teacher and coach both may join video-based lessons, or they may moderate students' comments so that more students receive feedback.
Micro Modeling	A portion of the lesson is modeled by the coach. The teacher and coach base their decision about what is modeled on the needs that have been identified by the teacher.	The coach teaches a video-based lesson so that the teacher can learn new strategies for teaching online. The coach can also join the class and deliver part of the lesson in synchronous learning.

MOVE 2: CO-ASSESS ACROSS PLATFORMS

Diane's daughter had been taking guitar lessons for more than five years when the virus closed her music school. Like many others, her teacher picked right up on Zoom, and they haven't missed a session since. As an online instructor, Will uses many high-leverage instructional practices. He gets her playing and then listens and assesses how she's doing. Then he gives her feedback about what she might work on next. This act of assessment is at the center of his teaching practice.

Now imagine an instructional coach telling Will that the first step in their work would be for the coach to model a lesson while Will sits by and observes. Remember, Will knows his students and understands where they are as learners—two areas where the coach would likely have very little insight. If another "teacher" took over Will's class to show him how it's done, you could just see those teenage eyes rolling now.

As it turns out, Will actually did reach out to another instructor for something that may loosely be defined as coaching. He was teaching a unit on Latin music and decided to integrate Spanish instruction. While Will speaks some Spanish himself, he recruited Anna, an elementary school Spanish teacher, to co-teach the lessons alongside him. Anna served as a co-assessor by joining the lessons in a way that still allowed Will to take the lead. They co-planned the lessons and identified what they hoped to hear from the students and how they would provide feedback. Anchoring their work in assessment created a seamless partnership where they worked side by side in a way that honored Will and integrated Anna's knowledge. When we envision co-teaching, this is what we see.

NOTICING AND NAMING

In *Student-Centered Coaching: The Moves* (Sweeney & Harris, 2017), we wrote a whole chapter on Noticing and Naming—it's that important:

> *Noticing* happens when a teacher and coach are actively tuned in and looking for evidence of student learning. *Naming* happens in the explicit use of this information, either on the spot or planning after the lesson, to make decisions about what the students need next. (p. 60)

The power in this move is that with a little norm setting, it can be used every time a coach is in another person's classroom. Few other moves are as universal as Noticing and Naming.

When we wrote this chapter a few years ago, little did we know we'd be transitioning to doing this virtually. The amazing thing is that coaches are finding that Noticing and Naming virtually is just as beneficial as it is in person. The primary reason for this, as we discussed in Chapter 3, is because we are collecting incredible amounts of student evidence in our LMS. Whether this consists of observational data collected by listening to student discussions or written work, we can use this evidence to anchor our conversations in formative assessment. There are so many opportunities for what a teacher and coach may choose to focus on when Noticing and Naming. This includes

- how students performed in comparison to the learning targets,

- the degree to which the students are engaging and participating as learners,

- how fluid the students are with any given technology,

- whether the students' responses indicate that they understand the content, and

- whether language is a barrier to the acquisition of learning.

We always emphasize that Noticing and Naming is anchored in the learning targets. That's because without criteria for what we want the students to know and do, this strategy becomes vague and less focused. Today, we recognize that much of our teaching is focusing on student engagement and the use of technology. This is why we are opening up the definition of Noticing and Naming to include engagement and behaviors as well. What's important is that the teacher and coach are clear about what they are looking for when using this move while co-teaching.

YOU PICK FOUR

We describe this move as a spinoff of Noticing and Naming. That's because You Pick Four is still very much focused on co-assessing and collecting student evidence. The difference is that it focuses on just a few students, rather than a whole class. We've all witnessed students falling through the cracks in the transition to online learning, and utilizing this co-teaching move can be a powerful way for a coach and teacher to get those students back on track.

You Pick Four can help create the conditions where we are more closely connecting with students who are struggling or disengaged or even with those advanced learners who may need an extra nudge. A coach may introduce this move with the simple question "Are there any students you would like me to keep an eye on?" This will likely surface a few students who would benefit from an additional layer of assessment. The coach can then focus on these students during the lesson and share the information that is collected.

CO-CONFERRING

There are lots of ways to formatively assess. One of the most powerful is through one-on-one conferences. In their text *Rigorous Reading*, Nancy Frey and Douglas Fisher (2013) write:

> Conferring provides the teacher with an excellent opportunity. These conferences allow the teacher to gauge the progress for each student, clarify information, and provide feedback for next steps. In addition, teachers keep records of these conferences for later reflection about individual student progress. (p. 117)

There is no reason why a transition to virtual learning means we should abandon this important practice for formative assessment.

During an in-person lesson, co-conferring means we pull up a chair next to a student to discuss how they are tackling their learning. We recommend that the coach and teacher do this together, instead of taking a "divide and conquer" approach. If we fan out to confer with different students, we lose the shared experience of deep conversations with the same student. This may diminish our opportunity to witness and learn from how the student engaged as a learner and for the teacher and coach to learn from one another. The approach of dividing and conquering also means that the teacher and coach may spend most of their time informing the other of what they heard, making it an inefficient strategy for co-assessing. When we co-confer, we are able to make decisions and address what the learner needs more quickly, sometimes right in the moment. We recognize that it may feel strange to suggest that two people working with one student is more efficient, but from a coaching perspective, we've found that this is indeed the case.

Co-conferring in a virtual setting is simply a matter of making the most of whatever technology you have at your fingertips. A low-tech way is to create a signup sheet in Google Docs for students to indicate a short block of time during office hours when they will join a Zoom or Google Meet with the teacher and coach. Another structure is for students to have a dedicated time each week when they participate in a conference. We can also poll students regarding their preferences for conferences. John Spencer (2020) writes:

> As an educator, you can honor student agency by asking them their preferences for check-ins. Students can submit their answers in an online form or in a short interview that you do at the beginning of the year. After students have submitted it, you can look at the spreadsheet and divide up your primary way of communicating with each student. This process sends the message that you value each student's input in their preferred approach to communication. As a result, they have a greater sense of control over frequency and method of communication. (para. 23)

Of course, we'd also advocate for the coach to be present during as many of these conferences as possible, because this ensures that the teacher has a co-assessor by their side.

Tool: Language for Co-Assessing

Noticing and Naming	"Which learning target would you like me to focus on when I'm collecting student evidence?"
	"What points in the lesson will allow us to collect the most evidence?"
	"Is there any specific language you'd like me to listen for?"
	"Have we planned enough opportunities for the students to demonstrate what they know using the available technology?"
You Pick Four	"Are there any specific students you'd like me to focus on when I'm Noticing and Naming?"
	"Can you tell me more about these students?"
	"Would you like me to listen in during whole-group, small-group, or one-on-one instruction?"
	"Let's be sure we come together to co-plan after I collect this evidence."
Co-conferring	"There's so much we can learn by doing conferences together. How about if I join you in some, so that we can really get a good sense of where your students are in their learning?"
	"What learning target would you like to focus on?"
	"How can we structure the conversation so that it's both efficient and informative?"
	"How would you like to take notes during the conferences?"

DISPATCH FROM THE FIELD

Amanda Brueggeman, Elementary Literacy Coach

When my coaching shifted online, I wanted to continue using the moves for Student-Centered Coaching. As a literacy coach in two elementary schools, my first hurdle was to help teachers get distance learning up and running. Next came questions about how I could continue to be efficacious as a coach. I decided to focus on co-planning and co-teaching as my primary strategies.

Heather, a special education teacher, and I decided to work on retelling with her first- through third-grade students. At our first virtual meeting,

(Continued)

(Continued)

I shared ideas about how we could partner together. She felt that our attention should be on the creation of the short video lessons that she would post weekly. We made a template of the lesson components and used it as we planned what we would include. Together, we also decided how we would share in the creation of each video.

An important part of our planning sessions was discussing how we would collect student evidence to gauge their understanding. Heather had already planned to use a survey she created in Google Forms, so we were ready to go on this part. Those data then drove our planning sessions and helped us decide on follow-up lessons. While we weren't sure how many retelling lessons we would need, the evidence made it clear that several students were struggling with how to describe the setting when retelling. With this information, we were able to become more targeted in the lessons that we taught through video.

Co-teaching in asynchronous lessons required us to plan the teaching point and how we could record it. We found a good system and stuck with it for all the video lessons that we co-taught together. With experience, we began to need to record the videos only once.

Synchronous co-teaching was the perfect time to use the Student-Centered Coaching move Noticing and Naming. To achieve this, we observed how the students were learning in response to the learning target. During another coaching session, when I worked with a teacher to design a virtual field trip to the San Diego Zoo, we observed student engagement and took notes focused on what students were doing, saying, and writing. We then used this evidence during a follow-up planning conversation, so that we could build in more strategic questions for the next lesson.

Using student evidence to help teachers decide on their next steps is still the most important aspect of my coaching. Pulling out tools such as note catchers and planning templates helps. I am often reminded that without co-planning, co-teaching is difficult. Recently, I was asked to join a class at the last minute, so I jumped right in. I quickly realized that I had no idea what my role would be, and I felt useless in the moment. Because our time with students is precious, it's important to be extra intentional in how we support teachers.

My immediate reaction during this transition was to not overwhelm teachers. I knew that they were worried about reaching their students while juggling technology in a limited amount of time. Offering to co-plan and co-teach helped me support them in meaningful ways.

MOVE 3: CO-DELIVER ACROSS PLATFORMS

How we co-teach depends on whether we are in a synchronous or asynchronous environment. What stays the same is that we still focus on what we know about high-quality instruction. For example, we want the students to engage in work that is both clear and challenging. We want to differentiate, so that the students' needs are met in a way that pushes them forward as learners. We also want to make those split-second decisions that are what responsive teaching is all about. While these are all possible in a remote learning environment, it may take a bit of reimagining to get there. We recommend the following coaching moves for co-delivering instruction in today's classrooms.

THINKING ALOUD

Thinking Aloud is a co-teaching move that increases the metacognition and reflection that happen throughout a lesson. It sounds something like this: "We just gave the kids a really tough question to grapple with in small groups. I'm going to be listening in to their conversations to make sure their struggle is staying productive and that they're not getting too frustrated." Metacognitive thinking about instructional decisions is shared in the moment to maximize learning opportunities for students and create openings for reflection and shared learning for the teacher and coach.

Co-teaching in a synchronous setting involves live lessons that are taught in person or on a screen. Typically, students are being introduced to new content or a process in these types of lessons. We've found that while teachers are getting more used to delivering instruction through a screen, it can still be hard to process everything that is coming at them at any given time. When your "students" are a grid of boxes that may not even have their cameras turned on, it can feel like you are teaching into a void. We must take this into account when Thinking Aloud during synchronous lessons, because teachers may not be ready for us to jump in and think aloud as they manage the lesson using a new technology. Instead,

Thinking Aloud may take place after the lesson concludes or during a break in the action, such as when the students are transitioning to breakout rooms. These moments provide a coach and teacher with the chance to check in on how learning is progressing without throwing teachers off their game.

TEACHING IN TANDEM

Teaching in Tandem is similar to team teaching. When co-planning the lesson, the coach and teacher strategically decide who will deliver the various parts of the lesson. Like the other co-teaching moves, Teaching in Tandem can take place during large-group, small-group, or one-on-one instruction. It is rarely an isolated practice and is commonly a part of the other co-teaching moves that have been outlined in this chapter. For example, in the Dispatch From the Field, when Amanda and the teacher worked together, they used the strategies of Noticing and Naming and Teaching in Tandem.

When teaching in person, you can envision Teaching in Tandem looking like the following image. The teacher and coach are both in the mix, thinking with students and each other. In this case, the coach is also doing some Noticing and Naming and Thinking Aloud as they discuss how the students might go about revising their writing. No stone is left unturned as the teacher and coach work through the instruction as thinking partners. The only difference is that when the lessons are taught virtually, the teacher and coach may not be in the same room doing this work.

MICRO MODELING

We use the term *micro* in the name Micro Modeling because the coach models only a small portion of the instructional block, rather than the whole lesson. This provides a visual example for teachers while also allowing the coach and teacher to share ownership over what is taught, something that is often missing when a coach is up in front of the room (or on the screen) teaching their heart out for an entire lesson.

When teaching asynchronously, many teachers are using Loom, Screencastify, or other applications to create instructional videos. This is one way in which coaches may support teachers through Micro Modeling.

Micro Modeling begins with a plan, so that the coach and teacher are able to narrow down what the coach will do and what the teacher will do during the lesson. This creates the opportunity for teachers to identify an area they would like to see a coach take on. The key is for this choice to be left up to the teacher if they want something to be modeled—and to decide what that something is. If we choose for them, we've effectively removed their teacher agency, which may undermine their buy-in and willingness to engage as a learner.

Tool: Language for Co-Delivering Lessons

Thinking Aloud	"I noticed _____. What I'm thinking is _____." "I think we might want to _____." "I'm wondering about _____." "When I see _____, it makes me think _____."
Teaching in Tandem	"What would you like to teach together?" "What parts of the lesson should each of us deliver?" When teaching online: "How can we use technology during the lesson?" "What if we _____?"
Micro Modeling	"I'm happy to micro model that part of the lesson. What pieces would you like to teach?" "I value what you bring to the lesson. Let's start there." When teaching online: "Can you tell me a little more about the videos we need to create for this unit?" When teaching online: "Are there tech tricks you need modeled? Like using breakout rooms or other features?"

Message From Coach Carrie

Dear Teachers,

Coaching is a partnership focused on student learning. Student-Centered Coaching cycles help guide this partnership.

Bottom line: I can't wait to spend time in your classroom to serve as a thinking partner. I won't be judging you or filling in an evaluation checklist. Mostly, I'll be kid watching and collecting student evidence, and I may even be a part of the lesson if you'd like. As we get started, we'll talk about a variety of co-teaching moves that we can use together. I can't wait to meet your kiddos.

In Learning,

Carrie

MOVE 4: MORE TIPS FOR CO-TEACHING

As we've discussed throughout this chapter, a big part of co-teaching is about supporting teachers in co-assessing, so that they can promote student learning. One of the ways we tackle this is by supporting differentiation in classrooms.

We know that differentiation is at the heart of all good teaching and learning, because no two learners are alike. While some students have transitioned to online learning without a hitch, others struggle with the executive function and organization skills that it requires. A parent of a student with an IEP writes, "Online learning is not a captivating solution for many students with ADD and learning disabilities, who struggle to grasp new concepts, stimulate attention, and finish work without teachers and specialists physically available" (Krum, 2020, para. 1). This message from a mother who has watched her daughter struggle is an important reminder that we need to think about how we might provide additional support, such as small-group and one-on-one instruction.

USING BREAKOUT ROOMS

Coaches can help teachers differentiate instruction by using breakout rooms. This includes the instructional focus, as well as the functionality of the breakout room feature. Breakout rooms allow us to better manage student check-ins or conferring sessions, which are at the heart of a well-differentiated classroom. The following tool provides planning questions for using breakout rooms.

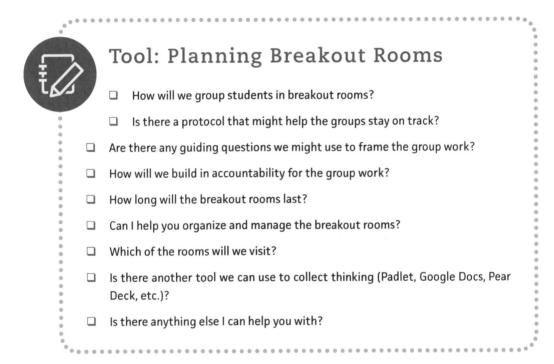

Tool: Planning Breakout Rooms

❑ How will we group students in breakout rooms?

❑ Is there a protocol that might help the groups stay on track?

❑ Are there any guiding questions we might use to frame the group work?

❑ How will we build in accountability for the group work?

❑ How long will the breakout rooms last?

❑ Can I help you organize and manage the breakout rooms?

❑ Which of the rooms will we visit?

❑ Is there another tool we can use to collect thinking (Padlet, Google Docs, Pear Deck, etc.)?

❑ Is there anything else I can help you with?

CO-PLAN BEFORE CO-TEACHING

Many of us have experienced the feeling of dropping into a lesson and having no real reason for being there. Being intentional about our work in classrooms helps us avoid these awkward moments. If our goal is to think with teachers about which instructional moves will have the greatest impact on student learning, we need to co-plan lessons on a regular basis. In doing so, we develop clarity around how instruction will progress and how the teacher and coach will share the responsibility for the lesson. This may sound time-intensive to a busy teacher, so we like to keep it simple. While we always make sure to co-plan the lessons we will teach together in mini or full coaching cycles, we may also find that we can co-plan lessons that we won't necessarily teach together. These practices were outlined in the previous chapter.

What Can We Carry Forward?

Nothing has changed when it comes to the fact that many teachers aren't used to having a coach in their classroom. This lack of clarity becomes even more pronounced when classes take place across virtual, hybrid, and in-person platforms. Reframing co-teaching takes us deeper into our partnerships with teachers. For this reason, we hope that the following practices persist long into the future:

- Always co-plan before co-teaching lessons.

- Remember that a coach can serve as a co-assessor, as well as a co-deliverer of instruction.

- Use tech tools to differentiate for students.

- Practice using "we" language, so that we don't take over the instruction but instead add to it.

CHAPTER 6

Coach for Rigor and Engagement

My son's teacher did a great job switching to distance learning. One thing I noticed is he was kept busy with work he could do on his own, but sometimes I wondered if it was challenging enough.

—Parent of a Sixth-Grade Student

How can we create the conditions for rigorous, open-ended, and engaging work for students? How do we nudge teachers away from busywork and toward opportunities for deep learning? These questions had been circling long before the shift to online learning, and now they can't be ignored. Students need to be able to work independently, and they need opportunities to engage in deep and meaningful learning. This is an issue of equity as much as it is of being able to successfully deliver instruction from a distance.

In *The Essential Guide for Student-Centered Coaching* (Sweeney & Harris, 2020), we shared a story of a time when we were coaching at an elementary school near a Native American reservation in southern Utah. What we witnessed were many students being assigned tasks that weren't challenging or interesting. This included word searches, books that were significantly below grade level, and packets of worksheets. Some of the students complied and did the work, and others caused overt or subtle disruptions throughout the school day. Some of the teachers worried that if the work was too hard, the students would act out even more. The school also lacked necessary materials, such as technology and robust classroom libraries. It was sad to see students with so much potential not being challenged or engaged. This experience started us on our journey to become student-centered, because we realized that if we can't work with teachers to mitigate these kinds of issues, what are we really here for?

MOVE 1: CREATE CONDITIONS FOR INDEPENDENT LEARNING

With teaching happening from a distance, it is critical to give students the tools they need to be able to learn independently. In Chapter 5, we discussed how coaches can help with this by partnering with teachers to create well-crafted lessons and units. But what do we really mean by independent learning, and what role do coaches play in this process? Let's take a look at the following examples.

A FIRST-GRADE LESSON

Violet is a first-grade student who loves her teacher, her classmates, and school in general. Since the fall, her school has been held remotely using Seesaw. Both of her parents work in a hair salon, and they have been trading off so that one of them is at home to help her navigate her learning.

During a recent science lesson focused on how to tell whether a snack is healthy, the teacher hoped the students would learn how to read labels so that they could see how many grams of sugar are in each serving. Then he planned to demonstrate how much sugar this really was. As he started the lesson, he asked the students to get a snack that they could show their classmates on the screen. Violet jumped out of her chair and asked her dad to help her find something. He found her a granola bar, and as the teacher continued to teach, Violet surreptitiously started to munch away. As the teacher glanced around at the students on camera, many were doing the same. Others didn't seem to have a snack at all.

When the lesson wrapped up, the teacher asked the students to post a short video about what they learned. Many said something like "It was fun" or "I liked my snack." None of the students mentioned how much sugar was healthy for them to eat. As the teacher listened, he realized that the learning targets he had in mind weren't met. He was happy they had fun but felt like he really missed the boat with the lesson as a whole.

HOW TO COACH INTO THIS SCENARIO

How might a coach have partnered with the teacher to help plan this lesson? One way would be to start the conversation by asking which learning targets the teacher would be focusing on. This is the first step in creating the conditions for students to know what they're supposed to be learning. Without this piece in place, the lesson became just a fun activity.

If we hope to provide opportunities for students to learn from a distance, they also need access to the learning itself. When planning this lesson, a coach may have questioned the assumption that every student could run and find a snack to share in the virtual classroom. What if some families are depending on food banks or come from a culture that doesn't eat the same foods as the other students? This could be not only embarrassing but also shameful for some of the students in the class. Through co-planning, the teacher and coach may have surfaced the idea of providing images of snack labels for the students to examine, instead of asking them to find one in their homes. To keep it fun, the teacher could have included some of the students' favorites, like Takis and Oreos. Then the lesson would have stayed focused on guiding the students to analyze the labels and notice the amounts of sugar in each one. Taking this approach would have been more equitable for all the students in the class, as it was likely that not everyone had a parent by their side who could hand them a granola bar.

Another key feature that a coach might surface is the importance of students demonstrating their understanding of the learning target. If the teacher was clear on the target and had shared it with students, it could have been directly aligned with the prompt for their videos. He asked them to "share what you learned about healthy snacks." While this prompt was nice and open-ended, it didn't connect to the intended learning about how to know whether or not a snack is healthy. Instead, the prompt could have been "When you read a snack label, what will you pay attention to?" along with "How does this connect to our learning target for today?" Taking this approach means the students are able to carry more of the cognitive load, leading them to go deeper in their thinking.

A HIGH SCHOOL EXAMPLE

Alex attends a school that is being held entirely online. He is an eleventh grader who is starting to look ahead toward graduation. He will be the first person in his family to attend college, and he knows that the higher his GPA is, the more likely he is to get a scholarship to help pay for his tuition. A lot is resting on his shoulders.

Because his school is being held remotely, Alex hasn't met his teachers in person and rarely has had the chance to interact with them. While he has been putting in the hours and trying to stay organized, he hasn't been getting much feedback about his work, especially in his chemistry class. In addition, he finds that the directions for assignments are confusing, and it's often unclear where to find the necessary materials within the LMS. With the final coming up, he decides that he'd better study extra hard, just to be safe. Juggling this with a part-time job means that Alex is getting just a few hours of sleep each night. Instead of using what little time he has to study in a way that is focused and productive, Alex begins to panic as he tries to cram every last detail from the unit. The lack of sleep and added anxiety end up affecting his ability to demonstrate what he really knows about the material.

HOW TO COACH INTO THIS SCENARIO

Clearly, Alex wanted to learn, but he didn't have all the tools he needed to do it from home. How might a coach have worked with his teacher to set up Alex and the other students for success? Partnering with the teacher to design accessible lessons within the school's LMS would have been a good starting point. Even in content-heavy subjects such as high school chemistry, where there is likely a set resource and curriculum, the switch to virtual instruction involves more than just moving lessons over to the LMS. A coach could have guided the teacher to think about how students would access materials and the wayfinding that could be built in to make expectations crystal clear to at-home learners, just as we discussed in Chapter 4.

A coach also could have supported the teacher by finding ways to give Alex and his classmates more information about how they're progressing. So much of our coaching model rests on formative assessment. When these levers are in place, students are able to make better decisions about how to spend their time because they know where they stand. Formative assessment wasn't a common practice for Alex's teacher, so Alex didn't really know how he was doing as a learner. All he had to go on were the points that were added to the student portal. When grading is only about points earned out of a total, we boil down learning in a way that will never support student independence. Imagine the difference if a coach had worked with Alex's teacher to

- create a clear progression for students to follow as they move through the content,

- co-construct formative assessments that align with each learning target, and

- design a system for providing feedback to students.

We acknowledge that if you've coached in a secondary environment, you have likely encountered the pushback that comes when we suggest that teachers ease up on grading. When coaches serve as thinking partners, they can help teachers work through these challenges. We see this not only as an opportunity for coaching but as a way to serve Alex and the rest of our students as well.

DISPATCH FROM THE FIELD

Mary Hendrickson Loeffler, Elementary Instructional Coach

When it was announced that our school district would be starting the 2020–2021 school year virtually, I immediately questioned how my role as an instructional coach could be leveraged to be more effective than it had been when we moved to distance learning at the onset of COVID-19. For the past few years, we have been studying and implementing universal design for learning strategies to meet the needs of our diverse learners. One of our school goals is for staff and students to be highly engaged learners who own the learning process. This goal aligns with Zaretta Hammond's work on moving students from dependent to independent learners. We held fast to the belief that we could continue our work on these goals, even through distance learning. My part in this would be to support teachers through Student-Centered Coaching.

The expectations for distance learning are that every week, teachers record a mini lesson in reading, writing, and math. Students also meet synchronously with their teachers in small groups for at least sixty minutes per week. At the time, I was actively coaching the fourth- and fifth-grade teachers who planned to start the year with new units of study in reading and writing. They selected units that would support their students after being away from school for several months. Two teachers from each grade level, a special education teacher, an English-language resource teacher, and I decided to work together in coaching cycles around these new units.

First, we read through the unit and established learning intentions based on the Common Core State Standards. We decided to keep the learning intentions focused on the skill of summarizing, which would support students' reading volume and comprehension. We also studied the Retelling/Summary/Synthesis strand of the learning progression provided by Teachers College Reading Units of Study (our adopted instructional resource). Then we developed success criteria based on the grade-level expectations. Next, we showed the students a short video that included a summary that we considered to be an exemplar. This step was important, as it painted a picture for students of what we expected them to include in their summaries. Students then co-constructed the success criteria with us during small groups by naming features that they noticed in the exemplar. Students then used the success criteria throughout the unit as they practiced summarizing books they were reading independently, books read aloud in class, and in response to videos they watched. They also used the success criteria to evaluate their summaries. This led to them giving each other feedback using Flipgrid. Students were encouraged to share their summaries verbally and in written form. Offering multiple means of expression lifted barriers and allowed students to be successful and more independent.

My work with these teachers enabled us to provide students with the conditions for independent learning. With clear expectations, success criteria that they created themselves, exemplars, and feedback, the students had what they needed to progress as learners. But the impact wasn't limited to the students. In fact, in our post-cycle conversations, the teachers indicated that they planned to continue this work in subsequent units.

MOVE 2: SELF-ASSESSMENT IS A MUST

As one of the core practices for Student-Centered Coaching, we always advocate for using student-friendly learning targets to create a road map for teachers. We also know that for formative assessment to be a truly high-leverage practice, we need mechanisms for students to self-assess and make decisions as they move through any given progression for learning. This is true now more than ever as we are teaching, learning, and coaching from a distance. Coaches can work with teachers to ensure that there are clear learning intentions and success criteria and that this information is shared with students (and their caregivers) in a way that is easy to access and understand. Coaches can also help teachers create rubrics and checklists, which are key tools for enabling students to work independently and assess their progress. The following examples illustrate how we can guide teachers and students to take these steps.

EXAMPLE FROM MIDDLE SCHOOL CIVICS

The first example was created by a middle school teacher and coach. They were partnering on an interdisciplinary unit that focused on the civil rights movement, in which students wrote a research paper as the culminating assignment. The rubric includes each of the learning targets, as well as what it looks like to reach the level of proficiency, or "meeting the target" (see Figure 6.1). Because this unit is now being taught virtually, each student has their own copy of the rubric in the LMS. That way, the teacher and coach can easily check in to see how students are progressing and can add comments and feedback where appropriate. Students who determine themselves to be "not there yet" on a given target can access a list of options for support. When a student determines that they are meeting or exceeding a given target, they are expected to provide evidence of why they believe this is so. They do this by cutting and pasting specific passages from their work or by indicating where to find it ("second paragraph of page 3," for example). Using a rubric like this allows students to assess where they are in relation to each of the targets and focus their attention where it's needed, without waiting for a teacher to direct them to resources or tell them what to do next. Being able to self-assess means they can direct themselves and take control of their own learning. A blank copy of each of the tools in this chapter can be found in Resource E.

FIGURE 6.1 ● Self-Assessment Rubric for Middle School Students

Intended Learning: *Students will analyze the role of a key figure within the civil rights movement.*

LEARNING TARGET	NOT THERE YET *Options for support:* • *Office hours* • *Exemplars* • *Video tutorials*	MEETS THE TARGET *Student provides evidence of meeting the learning target(s)* ***What it looks like to meet the target:***	EXCEEDS THE TARGET *Student provides evidence of exceeding the learning target(s)*
I can identify the ways in which my person gained power or effected social change in America.		• Describe the dream of my person. • Describe specific actions taken by my person during the civil rights movement. • Give specific examples of the methods my person used to effect change or gain power.	
I can analyze the reasons why my person chose a certain method of social change (violence, nonviolence, etc.).		• Identify the influences that led my person to choose certain methods of social change (family, mentors, life experiences, etc.). • Analyze how these influences affected the actions of my person.	

LEARNING TARGET	NOT THERE YET *Options for support:* • *Office hours* • *Exemplars* • *Video tutorials*	MEETS THE TARGET *Student provides evidence of meeting the learning target(s)* **What it looks like to meet the target:**	EXCEEDS THE TARGET *Student provides evidence of exceeding the learning target(s)*
I can evaluate the effectiveness of how my person gained power or effected social change.		• Provide specific examples of how my person's actions fulfilled their dream. • Evaluate specific actions to determine if they were successes or failures. • Describe my person's legacy: What did they leave behind? How did they affect society?	
I can express my thinking in the form of a research paper.		• Organize my paper around the central and supporting ideas of my research. • Write in a way that is clear and easy for the reader to understand. • Cite evidence that supports my claims. • Use appropriate spelling and conventions.	

Source: Sweeney, D. and Harris, L. (2017). *Student-Centered Coaching: The Moves.* Reprinted with permission.

EXAMPLE FROM AN ELEMENTARY ELL CLASS

In this example, a group of English-language learners are working on sharing an opinion using their speaking and writing skills. You'll notice that the structure of the self-assessment is similar to the previous rubric, with each of the learning targets identified down the left side (see Figure 6.2). Because these are younger students and second-language learners, there is a higher level of support in the description of what they can do at each of the levels of proficiency. This checklist is also used as an interactive piece where students write in their evidence ("I think cats are better than dogs," for example) in addition to creating the video. Again, this allows the teacher and coach to track and give feedback as the students progress toward acquisition of the learning targets.

FIGURE 6.2 ● Self-Assessment Checklist for Primary Students

Intended Learning: *Students will share an opinion that includes connected ideas.*

LEARNING TARGET	NOT YET *I need to practice or get help. I can get there by:* ● *Having a conference with my teacher.* ● *Practicing by making a recording.* ● *Listening to the examples.* ● *Watching the lesson videos.* ● *Practicing!*	ALMOST THERE *I just need a little more practice. I can get there by:* ● *Having a conference with my teacher.* ● *Practicing by making a recording.* ● *Listening to the examples.* ● *Watching the lesson videos.* ● *Practicing!*	YES! *I'm there, and here's my evidence:*
I can share an opinion about an animal, book, movie, etc.			
I can share why I have that opinion.			
I can use language stems: "I think . . . because. . . ."			

When teachers and coaches create the conditions for students to self-assess, it opens the door for them to take ownership over their learning and to have all the necessary tools to learn in a virtual, face-to-face, or hybrid learning environment. The following tool provides coaching language that can get us there.

Tool: Language for Coaching Into Self-Assessment

- Let's be sure we are crystal clear on what we want students to know and do and that we state everything in a way that students can understand on their own.

- How will we share the learning intention and success criteria with students?

- What kinds of supports need to be in place for students who aren't there yet on a target?

- What would we hope to see from students who have met each of the targets? Do we want to create exemplars for this?

MOVE 3: CULTIVATE INDEPENDENT LEARNERS THROUGH RIGOR AND ENGAGEMENT

Many educators are still working to define what it really means to create the conditions for independent learning. For some, this can be interpreted as packets of worksheets or self-paced units in an LMS. While it's true that these kinds of activities may lead to independence, do they lead to meaningful learning? We'd say probably not.

We became teachers in the era of constructivism, a theory of teaching and learning with the central idea that learning is constructed by building new knowledge on the foundation of previous learning, or schema. Because all students carry different schema, we struggled to find a way to make learning individualized and challenging. An example that comes to mind is how we taught Writer's Workshop some years ago. Students moved through the writing process at their own pace, and we tried to meet them where they were with the instruction that they needed. We carried a road map in our heads and hoped we could help students follow along, but this largely didn't happen. Instead, we found that we held the keys to the castle, and we never let our students in to find out what was expected.

Some of our colleagues decided that instead they would take their students step by step through the writing process with graphic organizers and other closed writing assignments that involved mostly copying what was being modeled. Most of the students complied, giving the teachers a false sense of success. While we took different approaches, what we had in common was that we weren't sure how to create the conditions for our students to develop as independent learners, much less to navigate the complexities of creating the conditions for rigorous and engaging learning to happen.

DEPENDENT VERSUS INDEPENDENT LEARNERS

An important aspect of our coaching role is to help teachers guide their students to be independent learners. This goes beyond students having the conditions to learn independently (such as with clear access to the materials and systems to self-assess); rather, it refers to a set of habits of mind and process strategies that students possess. Independent learners are problem solvers and deep thinkers who are equipped with strategies to engage in challenging learning tasks. Figure 6.3 shows how Zaretta Hammond (2015), author of *Culturally Responsive Teaching and the Brain*, defines the dependent and independent learner.

FIGURE 6.3 ● The Dependent Versus Independent Learner

THE DEPENDENT LEARNER	THE INDEPENDENT LEARNER
• Is dependent on the teacher to carry most of the cognitive load of a task always	• Relies on the teacher to carry some of the cognitive load temporarily
• Is unsure of how to tackle a new task	• Utilizes strategies and processes for tackling a new task
• Cannot complete a task without scaffolds	• Regularly attempts new tasks without scaffolds
• Will sit passively and wait if stuck until the teacher intervenes	• Has cognitive strategies for getting unstuck
• Doesn't retain information well or "doesn't get it"	• Has learned how to retrieve information from long-term memory

Source: Hammond, Z. (2015). *Culturally Responsive Teaching and the Brain: Promoting Authentic Engagement and Rigor Among Culturally and Linguistically Diverse Students.* Reprinted with permission.

Fostering independent learners primarily revolves around ensuring that students are carrying most of the cognitive load and that they have opportunities to engage in productive struggle. As Jo Boaler (2016) points out in *Mathematical Mindsets*, "the most productive classrooms are those in which students work on complex problems, are encouraged to take risks, and can struggle and fail and still feel good about working on hard problems" (p. 177). Coaches recognize that conversations around how to increase rigor and productive struggle can feel touchy, yet it is a critical part of our role to help teachers develop independent learners. The following tool lists some moves that coaches can take to help accomplish this.

Tool: Coaching Toward Independence

Coaches can support teachers in doing the following:

- ❑ Determine what learning needs to be scaffolded or, conversely, when too many scaffolds are in place.

- ❑ Create rituals and routines that provide students with the space to dig in first and, if needed, get help based on their specific needs.

- ❑ Model strategies to get unstuck. These may vary across face-to-face and remote learning environments.

- ❑ Use the Noticing and Naming strategy to watch for students who are struggling or stuck in a way that is no longer productive.

- ❑ Plan assignments that are challenging but also include the right number of scaffolds.

- ❑ Model language that promotes risk taking and a growth mindset.

GET CLEAR ABOUT ENGAGEMENT

It's common to hear the terms *engagement* and *classroom management* used interchangeably. We'd argue that just because a classroom is well managed doesn't mean students are engaged, and vice versa. Let's admit that the term *time on task* feels outdated when we are talking about opening up learning for our students. Let's also be honest that by now, many of our students know how to look engaged when they aren't. Teaching over webcam has only made that easier for them to pull off.

When entering the classrooms of others, either virtually or in person, it takes more than a glance or pop-in to determine whether students are engaged. We must look closely at the work they are doing, the conversations they are having, and how they are solving problems. All of this can be coached if—and only if—we are a part of the instruction that occurs in face-to-face or virtual classrooms. This is why co-teaching deserves a whole chapter in this book and a collection of moves to go along with it.

Part of the issue results from varying interpretations about what we mean when we talk about engagement. Perhaps the easiest type of engagement to foster is behavioral engagement, when students follow the rules, know how to play the game of school, and are often motivated by extrinsic factors, such as getting good grades or fear of getting into trouble. However, for students to be independent learners and to be successful in our current learning environment, we must create the conditions for two other types of engagement as well. The first is emotional engagement, which comes from feeling safe and known and having a sense of belonging. In Chapter 1, we explored ways coaches can work with teachers to build strong relationships with students and in turn enhance emotional engagement in our distance learning environment. The second is cognitive engagement, when students are invested in the learning and are intrinsically motivated by a need to know and the challenge of working on something they believe is relevant. This last type of engagement is perhaps the most difficult to achieve, which is why coaches can play such an important role in helping bring it about.

Message From Coach Carrie

Dear Teachers,

As your coach, I've gotten to see firsthand all the amazing work you are doing to support our students during this crazy time. I know many of us are feeling overwhelmed and vulnerable as we learn to adapt to our current reality. This includes me! Remember that my job is to partner with you to create meaningful learning experiences for *all* students. It may be hard to imagine what differentiation and small-group instruction look like right now, but I know we can figure it out together if we try.

Bottom line: I am a learner, too, and I believe that we are stronger together.

In Learning,

Carrie

MOVE 4: COACH TOWARD DEEP LEARNING EXPERIENCES FOR STUDENTS

Deep learning is possible, albeit challenging to make happen in today's environment. McTighe and Silver (2020) explain, "Students need content knowledge *and* process skills for rich learning experiences". The question then becomes this: How can coaches help teachers plan for both content knowledge and process skills when teaching virtually and in person?

In shifting to distance learning, much of the initial focus was on ensuring that the students learned the necessary content. We believe this was due to a few factors. The first is that teachers were worried about gaps showing up that would affect their students later once things resumed to "normal." We also noticed that it felt easier to add content-focused lessons to the LMS than to figure out how to create process-rich opportunities for learning. As a result, students spent a lot of time listening to teachers telling them what they should be learning through video or synchronous classes or working on what basically amounted to packets of digital worksheets. There is no question that it was challenging to find ways to get students to engage in processing and sharing their learning, but the longer this went on, the more disengaged some students became. Now that we've had more time to get comfortable with doing school from afar, it's time to retrain our focus on what matters most. Deep learning demands that educators create opportunities for students to engage with the content in ways that tap into their curiosity and problem-solving skills. This isn't easy to pull off with all the barriers that exist in distance learning, so that's where coaching comes in.

CREATE OPEN-ENDED LEARNING TASKS

Something that may hold educators back is the fear that loosening the reins may cause students to struggle. Though this mindset comes from a place of caring, it leads to over-teaching, over-explaining, and too much telling, and it keeps students locked in the "dependent learner" column. To understand whether we are creating the conditions for deep learning to occur, we can use this barometer: "Would I want to be a student in this classroom? And would I be challenged here?" To get there, coaches can work side by side with teachers to generate open tasks that are engaging, have multiple entry points, and create independent learners. Let's look at a few examples to see how they stack up.

EXAMPLE 1: LET'S MULTIPLY!

This example is visually interesting and has picture clues embedded for each problem. It also asks the students to show their work. Word problems are definitely a step up from a page of basic algorithms for kids to solve, so at first glance, it may appear that there would be deeper learning involved here. But looking closely, it's easy to see that if a student simply takes the two numbers in the problem and multiplies them, they can get the correct answer without reading a single word. Fun and eye-catching options such as this can lead us to believe that they involve more complex thinking than they actually do.

Name: _____ Date: _____

Class: _____ Teacher: _____

Let's Multiply!

Solve each multiplication word problem. Show your work.

 At Mya's school, 2 students dressed as skeletons in 3 of the classes. How many total skeletons were there?

 There are 8 houses on each block in Chantel's neighborhood. There are 4 blocks of houses. How many houses did she visit when trick-or-treating?

 Mario has 2 cats. He has 4 other neighbors that also have 2 cats. How many total cats are there?

 7 ghosts say 'Boo' to 6 children. How many children were scared?

Source: Author created using Canva Pro. www.canva.com

EXAMPLE 2: THE PIGS AND CHICKENS PROBLEM

This example requires students to use their problem-solving skills. It is totally open-ended, which means that teachers will be able to truly assess the students' understanding when analyzing the work that is created. There are also multiple entry points, so a student at any level would be able to give it a try. This type of task is great for pre- and post-assessment because at the beginning of a unit, students may be attempting to solve it by drawing a model. By the end, they could be given the same problem, and we would hope to see them solving it with a table or a system of algebraic equations, depending on the grade level.

Name: _____ Date: _____

Pigs and Chickens

Naomi owns a small farm where she raises pigs and chickens. She has 18 animal heads, and 50 animal legs. How many pigs does she have? How many chickens does she have? Be sure to show your work and your brilliant thinking!

Source: Author created using Canva Pro. www.canva.com

EXAMPLE 3: WRITING LEADS

Here, students are applying what they've been learning to craft leads for a narrative writing project. In this case, the students are combining content with process because they are expected to practice leads based on the previous instruction and then get feedback from a partner to select their best lead. In this task, learning is scaffolded through the success criteria, but students are also provided with a choice about how to tackle the learning.

Writing Leads

Today we will be practicing writing leads. Here's what we'll do as writers.

On a new page in your writer's notebook, add the date and title, "Leads".

Practice writing at least three leads for your personal narrative. Use the crafting techniques that we've been studying and remember that they are included on our success criteria.

Meet with your writing partner to share feedback about your leads. Select the one that you plan to use in your piece and put a star by it.

Source: Author created using Canva Pro. www.canva.com

HOW TO COACH DEEP LEARNING

The previous examples illustrate the importance of designing tasks that are rigorous and engaging. Coaches can support teachers in thinking critically about the type of work they are asking students to do and not getting fooled by cute and visually appealing options that may still require only low-level thinking. The following checklist of the qualities of open-ended learning tasks is useful for coaches when helping teachers assess the work they are asking students to do.

Tool: Checklist for Assessing Whether Tasks Lead to Deep Learning

❑ Students can think and solve problems in more than one way.

❑ Students are asked to share the strategies they used as learners.

❑ Information is applied in some way.

❑ Students are asked to think first.

❑ Students are able to decide how to approach the learning.

Source: Adapted from Fisher, Frey, and Hattie (2020).

Guiding teachers to assess their learning tasks with these criteria is a powerful act of coaching. If some of the qualities listed here aren't apparent in any given lesson, we'd recommend that the teacher and coach discuss whether this is okay and why. If several of the qualities are missing, it might be time to scrap the lesson and start over. Of course, a coach needs to approach these conversations with delicacy, so as not to judge the teacher, but we must find a way to have these discussions on behalf of our students. The following tool illustrates how coaches can accomplish this.

Tool: Language for Coaching Into Deep Learning

IF I HEAR . . .	THEN I CAN SAY OR DO . . .
"I found this fun activity on Teachers Pay Teachers. I think the kids are really going to love it!"	"This definitely looks like a lot of fun, and our students need that right now with being stuck at home. Let's look at this checklist to see if the activity has the qualities we would want to see, so that we can be sure it's asking them to do some deep thinking and problem solving."

IF I HEAR...	THEN I CAN SAY OR DO...
"I'm really struggling to keep up with this hybrid learning format, so I'll add some easy lessons to the LMS to keep the virtual learning students busy while I'm teaching the students who are face-to-face."	"Wow, concurrent instruction is really demanding a lot, and I appreciate all the hard work you're putting in. Maybe if the two of us can partner and work together on this, I can help you structure some meaningful learning for the asynchronous portion. That will help keep kids challenged and engaged, and they will come to the in-school lessons with you even better prepared."
"I know it's important to get kids to 'struggle,' but I worry about my students who will be doing this work on their own at home. They have such low skills, and I just don't know if they can handle it."	"I know how much you care about your students, and I agree that we need to give them work that they are capable of doing on their own without getting too overwhelmed and throwing in the towel. How about we look at some of these problem-solving tasks that are open-ended and have multiple entry points? That would allow all kids to access the material but still be challenged at their own level."

What Can We Carry Forward?

Let's admit it—nobody wants to be bored, and this includes our students. Designing rigorous work immediately pays off because it brings our students to the table in ways they may not have experienced in the past. In this chapter, you met some students and learned ways to coach into rigor and engagement. These practices aren't limited to the here and now, when things are happening from a distance. Rather, here are a few practices that will pay off long into the future:

- Design systems for students to self-assess as a way to create independent learners.

- Trust students to guide their own learning.

- Co-plan lessons that remove barriers for students to acquire content and learn processing skills.

- Be brave but respectful when having these coaching conversations.

CHAPTER 7

Building Partnerships in Challenging Times

I recently joined a virtual team meeting without having been invited. Only afterward did I realize that this felt really unnerving to some of the teachers.

—An Instructional Coach's Comment on Twitter

We've all been there before: we do something or say something with the best of intentions, but the look on the other person's face makes it clear that it did not land in the way we had hoped. What an uncomfortable feeling. This awkwardness and miscommunication can become even more apparent when working through digital platforms, where we don't have the benefit of in-person facial cues and body language. Strong, trusting relationships are a must for any coaching to be successful, and as many of us are now working from a distance, building these relationships is more important than ever. In our Student-Centered Coaching work, we recognize the intentionality that goes into building relationships and structuring partnerships so that they can function in a caring, professional, and effective way. This chapter addresses the moves we can take to do this with principals, teachers, and our fellow coaches.

In preparation for writing this book, we reached out to our coaching communities through social media and asked them what topics they would want to see addressed about coaching from a distance. Their feedback gave us many ideas that are woven through the preceding chapters, but the one thing that stood out above all others was the need to build trust and to nurture relationships during these challenging times. The rug has been pulled out from under us, both as educators and as a society at large. There are children and adults in our schools who are in freefall. Therefore, we need explicit ways to create and define partnerships that allow us to care for one another while working together to promote a rigorous, equitable learning experience in our schools.

DISPATCH FROM THE FIELD

Katie Shenk, Instructional Coach

Entering into a new role in a new school in a new district brings learning and challenges under normal circumstances, but beginning a new professional journey as an instructional coach in the pandemic has presented an even greater set of challenges—and opportunities. Because it's easy for me to get lost in the swirl, I strive to keep things as simple and manageable as possible. The current ever-evolving school landscape makes that more essential than ever; therefore, I named partnerships and presence as my "keepers" for the launch of this school year.

I knew from the start that I had to prioritize cultivating relationships with my school's instructional design team (administrators and my fellow coaches) in order to lay a solid foundation for myself as a new coach at the school. I am fortunate to have landed at a place where relationships between and among staff are valued and nurtured and we build in structures to ensure that staff feel connected, seen, and heard. We actively partner as an instructional design team to set and monitor schoolwide goals and to design professional learning opportunities to support progress toward our goals. Our partnership is anchored in trust, clarity of roles and responsibilities, and vulnerability. I've found that the latter is especially important right now. Our team openly shares challenges, puts innovative ideas on the table, and asks for help when we need it. Our honesty, innovative spirit, and collaboration have undoubtedly strengthened our partnership and, in turn, our ability to support teachers.

As a new coach at the school, I intentionally chose to use the first quarter of the year to be present for teachers as a cheerleader, thought partner, and lead learner. In the first few weeks of school, I prioritized getting into teachers' virtual classrooms to celebrate successes and get a pulse on challenges. I also supported beginning-of-the-year literacy assessments as a way to test-drive administering assessments remotely and to begin to get to know students in our school. Our coaching team leveraged weekly team co-planning meetings to continue to cultivate relationships with teachers through informal coaching and to be a support system for each other, too (as coaches, we need each other now more than ever). As a new coach, showing up as a fully present partner in learning has enabled me to build relationships with both the teachers and the leaders at my school. These foundational structures created the container for launching conversations about teaching and learning while simultaneously shining a light on my commitment to being a responsive and supportive instructional leader.

MOVE 1: PARTNER WITH THE PRINCIPAL

This move is one of our core practices for Student-Centered Coaching and one that we spend countless hours addressing in workshops, webinars, and conferences. Having a strong partnership with the school leader is critical to a coach's success, and we often say that this is what takes coaching "from good to great." When principals and coaches partner together, it can reap many benefits. Perhaps the most significant is that it leverages coaching to be an integrated part of the school's professional learning ecosystem. Instead of coaching being "one more thing" that teachers are asked to do, coaching is seen as a vital part of the overall plan to meet school improvement goals and support teacher learning. Furthermore, this partnership creates a culture where coaching can thrive. This is because the principal's support of coaching sends the message that we are all learners and that coaching is not about "fixing" teachers. Matsumura, Sartoris, Bickel, and Garnier (2009) found that teachers are more likely to participate in coaching when principals value and support coaches.

When building strong principal–coach partnerships, it's also critical to address how Student-Centered Coaching is a driver for equity. If the principal and coach share a vision for how coaching can support student achievement, they will be able to put the necessary pieces in place to get there. Without this vision, coaching may not serve students, especially if it is implemented in a relationship-driven or teacher-centered way. Coaching that fails to focus on student learning won't help us achieve equitable schools. It takes strong principal–coach partnerships for this to happen.

When coaching from a distance, this partnership becomes even more relevant, as our normal roles and routines may have changed dramatically since the onset of the pandemic. As we have settled in a bit more to our new normal, principals and coaches can shift out of the "triage trap" and begin to figure out what coaching should look like right now to best meet the needs of their school community.

DEFINE—OR REDEFINE—THE COACH'S ROLE

We have long advocated for the use of partnership agreements between principals and coaches. In the second edition of *Coaching Matters*, Killion, Bryan, and Clifton (2020) define this as

> a mutual agreement between the coach and the principal to define their working relationship and to establish the parameters of the coach's work, including responsibilities, limitations, and other details associated with the coach's work. A partnership agreement also includes the coach's expectations of the principal. (p. 101)

An example of a Principal and Coach Agreement can be found in Resource D.

Having an agreement in place allows us to frame discussions in an open and professional way. We all know that the sudden shift to remote learning in the spring of 2020 left many coaches in new and unchartered territory. Now that things have settled in a bit, it's probably a good idea to take stock of how the coach's time is currently being spent and to engage in an honest conversation about what their role should be right now. We want to emphasize the words *right now* because this moment is calling on us to strike a balance between addressing the unique needs of our current circumstances with what we know to have the biggest impact on student achievement. *Right now* a principal and coach may determine that the coach's role should include working with small groups to help with distancing requirements, for example. When these requirements are no longer in place, we would expect a coach to return to more co-teaching when in classrooms. The following tool offers scenarios and language that principals can use to define the coach's role and how it may look a little different during this time.

Tool: Language for Defining Coaching Right Now

IF WE HEAR OR NOTICE...	THEN THE PRINCIPAL CAN SAY OR DO...
The coach is teaching two sections of ELA to keep class sizes low. This has led many teachers to believe that the coach is no longer coaching. They are asking her to do all sorts of things, from covering classes to distributing hand sanitizer to classrooms.	The principal can explain to the staff that the coach is taking on these teaching duties temporarily, and the expectation is that the rest of the coach's time will be spent coaching.
Teachers are reaching out to the coach for a lot of tech help, but no one seems interested in moving into deeper work.	The principal may say, "Our coach has been spending a lot of time helping you get comfortable with the LMS, which has been a great asset. Don't forget that he's also available for mini and full coaching cycles. Many of you seem ready to jump into that, so be sure to let him know if you're interested."
Teachers are working hard to figure out how to deliver high-quality instruction online, but many are finding it to be a challenge. Because they feel so vulnerable and stressed, few have thought to reach out to the coach for help.	The principal may say, "I know it's hard to imagine how our coach could partner with you in a virtual lesson, but she was just sharing some of her experiences with me yesterday, and it sounds really powerful. Definitely reach out to her if you want to learn more."

Another aspect of the coaching role that has come into the spotlight relates to technology. As we've discussed, this can be a tricky area, because some tech coaches may want to coach but find themselves mostly giving tech support, and others want to be the tech resource person but are expected to coach. The pivot to remote learning caused all coaches to take on a much more prominent role regarding technology. Now that the "SOS" phase is behind us, we believe that principals and coaches need to be thoughtful about expectations around the coach's role with technology. Again, having an agreement in place will help these conversations happen. Our hope is that coaching conversations are centered around student learning, while looking at ways in which technology can be used to both enhance and transform that learning.

CONTINUE TO ADVOCATE FOR COACHING

With coaches working from home or in school buildings where there are still limitations on how they can interact with others, it can be challenging to connect with teachers to find openings for coaching. The principal can have a big influence here by being a strong advocate for the coach and the coaching work. When meeting with grade-level or department teams, professional learning communities (PLCs), or individual teachers, a principal can have an eye open for potential partnerships for the coach. Remember that this does not mean that the principal is looking for problems that the coach must then go fix; rather, the principal is "singing the praises" of coaching to teachers and helping connect those who are interested with the coach.

Coaches depend on these messages from the principal. For example, some teachers who have engaged in coaching cycles in the past may now be saying they don't want to work with the coach because it feels like too much to engage in a full coaching cycle. To honor this concern, the principal may remind teachers that they can also elect to work with a coach during unit-planning sessions or PLCs. This provides teachers with a thinking partner and may also create future openings for further coaching down the line.

One thing that makes the principal–coach partnership reach its full potential is setting time aside each week to meet. This is no different whether school is happening remotely or in person. Regular meetings ensure that both parties are supporting one another, that they can continually revisit and redefine the coach's role during this time, and that together they can work to engage teachers in coaching.

MOVE 2: PARTNER WITH TEACHERS

Building trusting relationships with teachers takes a lot of time and effort in the best of circumstances. As student-centered coaches, we work hard to help teachers understand our beliefs about coaching: that we are partners, rather than evaluators; that we do not have all the answers, but we want to figure it out together; and that moving student learning forward is at the heart of every coaching conversation. Now, with teachers overworked, feeling vulnerable, and in many cases still working remotely, the challenge of relationship building has grown. We've heard these questions a lot over the past several months: "How do I get teachers to invite me to their team meetings?" "How do I engage teachers?" and "How do I get teachers to see me as a valuable resource and partner?" We believe one of the most meaningful things a coach can do right now is to start with a bottomless supply of grace, compassion, and humility. Student-Centered Coaching has never been about "fixing" teachers, but now we need to work even harder to ensure that we are not judging or taking on an evaluative role.

We do this by

- assuming best intent (everyone is trying their hardest to do right by their students);

- taking an asset-based approach with teachers (focus on all the good things they are doing, instead of the things they are not doing);

- keeping teachers in the driver's seat, rather than coaching to our own agenda;

- providing feedback that is strengths-based and created through reflective dialogue; and

- not overwhelming teachers with too many of our own ideas.

The good news is that this is all about the "what" and not about the "how." In other words, our disposition and our messaging are the same whether we're in a virtual setting or in person. Perhaps the biggest difference right now is that we simply need more: more grace, more compassion, and more humility—more messaging that lets teachers know that we've got their backs, that these are *our* students, and that *together* we can make a positive impact on student achievement.

SET CLEAR EXPECTATIONS THROUGH NORMS AND AGREEMENTS

When trusting relationships have been established and teachers are ready to engage in coaching, the natural temptation is to jump right in and get going. But we know from our own past mistakes, and from many coaches we've seen stumble, that this is the time to remember the mantra "You've got to go slow to go fast." Teachers who don't spend time at the beginning of the year to build a classroom community with clear expectations and shared commitments often end up wasting hours of instructional time addressing behavior issues later in the year. Coaches who don't work with their principal to define their role and their expectations for each other often end up wearing a lot of different hats that have nothing to do with coaching. So it is in the teacher–coach partnership. If the time isn't put in up front to establish norms and expectations, the train can easily lose steam and go off track.

When engaging in unit planning, lesson planning, or mini coaching cycles, the work is short enough in duration that it may not warrant filling out a full Partnership Agreement for a Coaching Cycle (which can be found in Resource D). However, it's always important to get on the same page before beginning the work by taking the time to discuss a few key items, such as those listed in the following tool.

Tool: Language for Partnering With a Teacher

- Would you like to co-plan a lesson or unit or engage in a mini coaching cycle?
- What learning will we focus on?
- Is this being taught synchronously or asynchronously?
- Is there anything you want me to know about your students, circumstances, and so on?
- Is there anyone else you'd like to include in the work (special ed, ELL, district coach, tech coach)?

Remember that coaching is built on relationships, so we don't mean to imply that this should be a stiff and formal process. It's just about being intentional and not assuming that everyone is automatically on the same page. Having these conversations on the front end sets us up for productive, respectful, and successful coaching partnerships.

The following tool walks through the steps for enrolling teachers in coaching cycles. Whether you're working with teachers at this level of coaching or not, we hope this will be a useful tool to guide you toward engaging teachers in coaching. Building relationships, being present, and getting clear on shared expectations will help us rise to the challenge of this moment by supporting teachers and partnering with them to provide high-quality learning experiences for students.

> ### TOOL: STEPS FOR ENROLLING TEACHERS IN COACHING CYCLES
>
> 1. **Build Relationships by Connecting With Teachers in Person and Virtually**
>   - Introduce yourself to the staff (whole staff, teams, and individuals) virtually and/or in person.
>   - Help with beginning-of-the-year tasks, such as classroom setup, technology, assessments, and so forth.
>   - Provide resources to teachers for virtual or in-person teaching.
>
> 2. **Listen for Openings**
>   - Find openings when coaching informally, such as co-planning lessons and units.
>   - Attend existing meetings, such as PLCs, department meetings, or those for grade-level teams.
>   - Invite teachers to participate, or ask if they will help you "practice" something new.
>
> 3. **Set Norms and Agreements**
>   - Define clear expectations for the coach and teacher.
>   - Discuss how you will work together (this may vary, depending on whether it's happening virtually or in person).
>   - Schedule times each week for co-planning and co-teaching.
>   - If school shifts from remote to in person, or vice versa, plan how coaching will be adjusted.
>   - Create a shared folder for all coaching documents, such as the Results-Based Coaching Tool and coaching logs.
>
> 4. **Launch Coaching Cycles**
>
> *Source:* Adapted from Flaherty (2010).

MOVE 3: PARTNER WITH OTHER COACHES

With coaches being called on to have an abundance of grace, compassion, and humility, it begs the question: "Who is taking care of *us* right now?" We are typically the ones who jump in and help our principal where needed, we strive to be supportive of teachers, and we care deeply about the students in our schools. But as coaches, we must also recognize our own need for support and care, both personally and professionally. While many coaches receive this from their principal, district leader, and other colleagues at their school, we have an important and often underutilized resource right in front of us, which is our fellow coaches.

LEVERAGE YOUR PROFESSIONAL LEARNING COMMUNITY OR NETWORK

The most obvious way for us to partner with our fellow coaches is by creating a PLC with the other coaches in our school or district. Many coaching teams have an administrator who leads the coaching effort, and teams in these cases typically meet regularly for training around pedagogy, curriculum, and other initiatives. This kind of support helps coaches build their expertise around content and all the other "stuff" that happens in schools, but it typically doesn't often offer guidance on how to be a coach. Therefore, coaches may find they need another way to get this kind of support.

Just like teachers, coaches can benefit tremendously from working together in a PLC. This is a place for shared professional learning, like a book study, for example. It is where coaches receive feedback on problems of practice, and it is also a place to work on collective problem solving around shared issues of focus or concern. While it's nice when these meetings can take place in person, many coaching PLCs have made the smooth transition to meeting virtually and are even finding that it's easier to schedule when they don't have to account for travel time. As with all PLCs, the use of protocols is recommended to keep the work productive and on track. The following tools include a Consultancy Protocol and a Protocol for Providing Strengths-Based Feedback, which are useful resources for helping individual group members work through and get feedback on a specific dilemma in their coaching work. While the protocols are similar, we provide both to illustrate the nature of these conversations.

TOOL: CONSULTANCY PROTOCOL

Purpose: This protocol is used to explore a problem or dilemma related to coaching.

Suggested time: 45 minutes

Roles:

- **Presenting coach** shares a dilemma for the group to discuss.
- **Participants** listen, reflect, and discuss the dilemma that is shared.
- **Facilitator** manages the process, keeps an eye on the time, and encourages everyone to participate in the discussion.

Process:

1. The presenter shares an issue or dilemma from their coaching work. If possible, the issue is presented in the form of a focus question (3–5 minutes).

2. The facilitator restates the issue or dilemma to ensure that it is clear and well understood (1–2 minutes).

3. Participants ask clarifying questions to be sure they understand the context and history of the issue or dilemma. The presenting coach responds to the questions to provide more context and background (5 minutes). (*Note:* Clarifying questions are aimed at helping the participants understand the issue or dilemma and are not a place to make suggestions.)

4. Participants ask probing questions. The presenting coach responds to the group's questions to continue adding context and background (5–10 minutes). (*Note:* Probing questions are deeper than clarifying questions but still are not suggestions. They are intended to spur reflection and possibility thinking.)

5. The presenting coach listens and takes notes while the participants discuss the issue or dilemma that was presented (5–10 minutes).

6. The presenting coach responds to the discussion and thoughtfully reflects on their next steps (5 minutes).

Source: Adapted from the National School Reform Faculty.

TOOL: PROTOCOL FOR PROVIDING STRENGTHS-BASED FEEDBACK

Purpose: This protocol is used to explore a problem or dilemma related to coaching.

Suggested time: 45 minutes

Roles:

- **Presenting coach** shares a dilemma for the group to discuss.
- **Participants** listen, reflect, and discuss the dilemma that is shared.
- **Facilitator** manages the process, keeps an eye on the time, and encourages everyone to participate in the discussion.

Process:

1. **Review the Protocol and Norms (5 minutes)**

   - The facilitator sets the stage for the learning and shares the following norms:
     - Assume positive intent throughout the conversation.
     - Listen and take notes.
     - Follow the protocol so that the conversation stays on track.

2. **Share a Problem of Practice (10 minutes)**

   - The presenting coach provides background about their recent coaching work.
   - The presenting coach shares a pressing challenge or issue.
   - Participants ask clarifying questions, so that the fuller picture is understood.

3. **Value (5 minutes)**

   - A few participants celebrate something they heard from the presenting coach.

4. **Uncover Possibilities (15 minutes)**

   - The presenting coach and participants brainstorm ideas that will support the coach in moving the work forward.

Source: Adapted from Sweeney and Harris (2020). Used with permission.

REACH OUT TO A PROFESSIONAL LEARNING NETWORK (PLN)

While PLCs are a great structure for coaches to support one another, the reality is that not every coach is part of a bigger team. A silver lining of this pandemic is that it has broken down the barriers of physical space. People are attending classes, meetings, and events from anywhere that are taking place nowhere. This is something that most of us would never have imagined just a short time ago. For years, coaches have been active on various social media platforms as a way to connect with colleagues for support and feedback. As we all continue to learn and grow in this digital space, what better time to tap in to a professional learning network (PLN) of fellow coaches from literally all over the world?

We can also take advantage of the opportunities that have been opened for collaborating via technology. Many coaches are lamenting the loss of coaching labs this year, but that hasn't stopped them from learning from one another through observation. In pairs or small groups, coaches have been sharing videos of their co-planning and co-teaching sessions (with teachers' permission, of course) to create experiences much along the lines of the coaching labs that would normally take place in person. For more on coaching labs, check out *The Essential Guide for Student-Centered Coaching* (Sweeney & Harris, 2020).

NORMS AND AGREEMENTS STILL MATTER

Even though many of the ways we collaborate with each other as coaches are collegial and informal in nature, it's still important to consider how norms and agreements can help our work be professional and productive. Observing colleagues, as we just discussed, is definitely a situation where we want to be sure that norms are in place. When working together as a PLC, we should also begin by setting norms. These shared commitments are set by the group and guide members in working together. They help clarify expectations for how a group will work and communicate in order to support one another and reach shared goals. Anyone who's done training on or been in a PLC knows how important this is for teachers. The same holds true for teams of coaches.

Coaches may also find themselves collaborating when district-level coaches (or specialists) are working in schools where there is also a site-based instructional coach. The district coach may be coming in to support teachers around technology, social-emotional learning, special education, English-language acquisition, behavior, or a specific content area. We've seen many powerful partnerships between these specialist coaches and the school-based, student-centered coaches over the years. Yet we've also witnessed some that become messy and even tense because the understanding of roles and expectations seems to be at odds between the two coaches. Instead of giving a teacher a powerful, coordinated, double dose of support, this can leave a teacher with mixed messages and feeling pulled in two directions. This is the last thing we want to have happen, especially now, when teachers are overburdened and need all the help they can get. So in these cases, when a district coach will be working at the same school as a site-based coach, we recommend using an agreement and bringing the principal into these conversations as well. Just as with principals and teachers, having agreements with our fellow coaches enables us to work in a way that is much more productive and beneficial to the teachers we serve. The following tool provides some of the questions we believe are helpful to discuss.

Tool: Language for Partnering With Another Coach

- As a district coach, how can I collaborate with the coaching that's happening in your school?

- I would like to coordinate with you and the principal to make sure we're all on the same page. When would be a good time to join one of your meetings?

- How can we support each other's coaching work?

- What is your plan for messaging coaching? Is there a way to include both of us in this?

- When does it make sense to partner in a cycle?

- What is our plan for communication?

Many coaches are caregivers by nature who thrive on serving others. What a beautiful thing that is. Yet it's important to remember that we still need to tend to our own emotional support and professional growth, and for this, we can rely on our relationships and partnerships with fellow coaches.

Message From Coach Carrie

Dear Teachers,

Coaches are *not* administrators.

Coaches are partners working in the classroom with teachers and students. Coaches do communicate with administrators about the work they are doing in teachers' classrooms. However, the main information coaches share with administrators is around student-centered goals. This communication is not tied to teacher evaluation in any way, shape, or form. Instead, it is used to make sure that the coach is held accountable for the work they are doing.

Bottom line: I am on the same playing field as you. I am your partner in promoting and facilitating student learning. If you see me talking to . . .

Mr. Casey or Ms. Hickman, assume we are discussing his love for the Patriots, her love of running, and my disdain for one of those things.

Ms. Teague, assume we are discussing the new Sonic that's coming to Clever. Trust me, it's been in the works for years.

Ms. Hobbs, assume we are discussing her love of running and my love of donuts.

Mr. Sullivan, assume we are discussing the age-old rivalry of the Cardinals versus the Cubs.

In Learning,

Carrie

MOVE 4: NURTURE YOUR SCHOOL CULTURE

Most of us have experienced feelings of isolation in some way during this pandemic. From being told to "shelter in place" in our homes, to not being able to connect in person with friends and family members, to missing out on our favorite social activities, such as sporting events or the theater, this time has left us longing to connect with others. Building and maintaining partnerships with principals, teachers, and fellow coaches is a big part of the way we can do this in our professional lives, and it is a critical component of our ability to have efficacy in our work. We must also remember that each of these partnerships does not exist in a bubble. Together, along with our students, their parents and caregivers, and other staff members, we are a part of the same school community. The culture of these school communities to which we belong has taken a hit. Some school buildings continue to be closed, while others are full of people who must stay six feet apart. Some students have been hard to track down. Many community members have lost loved ones in the pandemic.

In our work advocating for Student-Centered Coaching, we often get to collaborate with district and school administrators. We try to impress on them the need to create the space for coaches to spend the majority of their time partnering with teachers on goals for student learning. Our belief is that this is the way for coaches to have the biggest possible impact in their work. In this book, our hope has been to stay true to that belief while at the same time addressing the challenges, complexities, and opportunities that have been presented in this moment. So when we talk about "nurturing the school culture," this is not to imply that we believe it's the coach's job alone to tackle this leviathan task. Rather, we would like to end with a reminder of the shared responsibility and benefit that come with being a part of a community and the culture it lives within.

Where Do We Go From Here?

In each chapter, we have shared thoughts about what we hope will carry forward from this collective experience to make schools more innovative and more equitable. We are all on this incredible journey together, and amid the challenge and loss, we have forged extraordinary new paths forward. As we think about the amazing community and culture that live within our schools, our hope is that the following questions will continue to be addressed as we move through and beyond this pandemic: How can we build a supportive culture around mental health and well-being? How can we continue to build our collective efficacy? And finally, how can we fill our schools—whether in person or at a distance—with as much joy as possible? These are big questions, but we know one thing for sure. We will find the answers as coaches, together in partnership with teachers, principals, students, and their families.

Resource A

Results-Based Coaching Tool

RESULTS-BASED COACHING TOOL

Coach Name:

Teacher Name(s):

Dates of Coaching Cycle:

Coaching Focus (Grade/Subject/Content):

Standards-Based Goal	Instructional Practice	Instructional Coaching	Teacher Learning	Student Learning
What is the goal for student learning?	What instructional practices will help students reach the goal?	What coaching practices were implemented during this coaching cycle?	As a result of the coaching, what instructional practices are being used on a consistent basis?	How did student learning increase as a result of the coaching cycle?
Students will . . .	**Teacher will . . .**	**Coach and teacher did . . .** (check all that apply)	**Teacher is . . .**	**Students are . . .**
		☐ Goal setting		
		☐ Creating learning targets		**Student Learning**
		☐ Analysis of student work		How did student learning increase as a result of the coaching cycle?
		☐ Co-teaching		
Standard(s):		☐ Collecting student evidence during the class period		**Post-Assessment Data:**
		☐ Collaborative planning		____ Emerging
		☐ Shared learning to build knowledge of content and pedagogy		____ Developing
Learning Targets:				____ Meeting
I can:		**Other:** _____		____ Exceeding
		_____		____ % of students were able to demonstrate proficiency of the learning targets

Baseline Data:

_____ Emerging

_____ Developing

_____ Meeting

_____ Exceeding

_____% of students were able to demonstrate proficiency of the learning targets

Follow-up for students who didn't reach the goal:

(Continued)

(Continued)

TEACHER REFLECTIONS	COACH REFLECTIONS
How did the coaching cycle support the students' learning?	What coaching moves most supported the coaching cycle?
Were there any challenges or missed opportunities during the coaching cycle?	Were there any challenges or missed opportunities during the coaching cycle?
What are some next steps for your teaching as a result of the coaching cycle?	What are some next steps for your coaching as a result of the coaching cycle?

Source: Sweeney, D. and Harris, L. (2020). *The Essential Guide for Student-Centered Coaching.* Reprinted with permission.

online resources ⚡ Available for download from **resources.corwin.com/SCCFromaDistance**

Copyright © 2021 by Corwin Press, Inc. All rights reserved. Reprinted from *Student-Centered Coaching From a Distance: Coaching Moves for Virtual, Hybrid, and In-Person Classrooms* by Diane Sweeney, Leanna S. Harris. Thousand Oaks, CA: Corwin, www.corwin.com. Reproduction authorized for educational use by educators, local school sites, and/or noncommercial or nonprofit entities that have purchased the book.

THE RESULTS-BASED COACHING TOOL DECONSTRUCTED AND ANNOTATED

Standards-Based Goal

What is the goal for student learning?

Students will . . .

◀ Using the language "students will" helps us stay focused on the fact that our goal is about learning rather than a teaching strategy or structure.

Standard(s):

◀ Sometimes a goal will align specifically with one particular standard; often several standards or parts of standards are addressed at once.

Learning Targets:

I can:

◀ The goal is broken down into a set of learning targets, or success criteria, which will guide instruction throughout the coaching cycle and which will be used to formatively assess along the way.

Baseline Data:

_____Emerging

_____Developing

_____Meeting

_____Exceeding

_____% of students were able to demonstrate proficiency of the learning targets

◀ A pre-assessment is given in order to determine baseline data and to see what understanding students are already bringing to the learning. The descriptors can be modified to match specific school or district language.

Instructional Practice

What instructional practices will help students reach the goal?

Teacher will . . .

◀ This section is where thinking is held about all the strategies, structures, resources, and activities that might be used throughout the coaching cycle in order to help students reach the goal. This can include things the teacher says they want to work on (e.g., setting up a readers' workshop), as well as school or district expectations (such as implementing the new math curriculum). The list can be added to as new thinking is generated throughout the coaching cycle.

(Continued)

(Continued)

Instructional Coaching

What coaching practices were implemented during this coaching cycle?

Coach and teacher did . . .

(check all that apply)

- ❑ Goal setting
- ❑ Creating learning targets
- ❑ Analysis of student work
- ❑ Co-teaching
- ❑ Collecting student evidence during the class period
- ❑ Collaborative planning
- ❑ Shared learning to build knowledge of content and pedagogy
- ❑ Other _____

◄ Here the coach can keep track of all of the different ways they collaborate with the teacher(s) during the coaching cycle. It also serves as a way to help teachers understand what to expect the coach to be doing (and not be doing) in a cycle.

Teacher Learning

As a result of the coaching cycle, what instructional practices are being used on a consistent basis?

Teacher is . . .

◄ This is where the teacher can reflect on their own learning and growth as a result of the coaching cycle. It can be generated from time in the classroom or from reflection at the end of the coaching cycle. It is important to note that this is not a place for evaluation but rather for celebration. Most of the thinking should come from the teacher.

Student Learning

How did student learning increase as a result of the coaching cycle?

Students are . . .

◄ Anecdotal evidence can be shared about how students have grown in their learning and can be recorded here. It may be specific to the learning targets, or it may be more general, such as reflections about an increased level of student engagement.

Post-assessment Data:

_____Emerging

_____Developing

_____Meeting

_____Exceeding

_____% of students were able to demonstrate proficiency of the learning targets

⬅ The post-assessment should mirror the pre-assessment as closely as possible in order to adequately measure growth.

Follow-up for students who didn't reach the goal:

⬅ There may be a few students who didn't yet reach the goal. It is important for the coach and teacher to make sure a plan is in place to continue to support these students with the learning.

Source: Sweeney, D. and Harris, L. (2020). *The Essential Guide for Student-Centered Coaching.* Reprinted with permission.

 Available for download from **resources.corwin.com/SCCFromaDistance**

Copyright © 2021 by Corwin Press, Inc. All rights reserved. Reprinted from *Student-Centered Coaching From a Distance: Coaching Moves for Virtual, Hybrid, and In-Person Classrooms* by Diane Sweeney, Leanna S. Harris. Thousand Oaks, CA: Corwin, www.corwin.com. Reproduction authorized for educational use by educators, local school sites, and/or noncommercial or nonprofit entities that have purchased the book.

Resource B

Coaching Cycle Logs

MINI COACHING CYCLE LOG

COACHING LOG: MINI COACHING CYCLE	
Teacher:	Grade/Subject:
Coach:	Dates of Cycle:

1. What is the goal or target? What bigger learning does it sit under?

2. What evidence do we have, or need, that will inform us of where students are?

3. Based on our evidence, what did we learn, and what can we try?

4. How will we co-deliver instruction?

5. How did the students do? What are some next steps for instruction?

 Available for download from **resources.corwin.com/SCCFromaDistance**

Copyright © 2021 by Corwin Press, Inc. All rights reserved. Reprinted from *Student-Centered Coaching From a Distance: Coaching Moves for Virtual, Hybrid, and In-Person Classrooms* by Diane Sweeney, Leanna S. Harris. Thousand Oaks, CA: Corwin, www.corwin.com. Reproduction authorized for educational use by educators, local school sites, and/or noncommercial or nonprofit entities that have purchased the book.

COACHING LOG: SET STANDARDS-BASED GOALS

Guiding Questions:

1. What is the goal for student learning for this coaching cycle? What do we hope the students will learn as a result of our partnership?
2. Are there any data that will inform us as we set a goal?
3. What standard(s) does this goal address?
4. Is there a specific unit in the curriculum that the goal addresses?

Notes and Next Steps:

COACHING LOG: UNPACK THE GOAL INTO LEARNING TARGETS

Guiding Questions:

1. What are the learning targets (or success criteria) that will help the students reach the goal?
2. Do the learning targets address a balance of *know*, *understand*, and *do*? Do they go beyond lessons and activities?
3. Are there any behavior targets that we want to include?
4. Are the targets written in student-friendly language?

Notes and Next Steps:

COACHING LOG: CREATE A PLAN FOR THE PRE-ASSESSMENT

Guiding Questions:

1. How will we assess the students to measure growth across the coaching cycle? We can use an existing assessment or create our own.
2. Is the assessment open-ended and descriptive in nature?
3. Does the assessment align with the learning targets?
4. When will we meet again to analyze the data that we collect?

Notes and Next Steps:

COACHING LOG: DOCUMENT BASELINE DATA

Guiding Questions:

1. How did the students perform on the pre-assessment?

% EMERGING	% DEVELOPING	% MEETING	% EXCEEDING

2. Do the data indicate any ways in which we should modify or prioritize the learning targets? If so, how?
3. Based on the data, what is our first step in instruction?

Notes and Next Steps:

COACHING LOG: CO-PLAN WITH STUDENT EVIDENCE

Guiding Questions:
1. What is the learning target for the lesson?
2. How will students demonstrate their understanding of the target?
3. How would we want students to answer the following questions?

- What am I learning?
- Why am I learning it?
- How will I know when I have learned it?

4. Do we have evidence from the last lesson that will inform how we can differentiate instruction?
5. What resources and materials will we need to prepare?
6. How will we work together to manage student behavior?

Planner for Sharing Lessons

WHAT'S HAPPENING?	WHAT WILL IT LOOK LIKE?	WHO WILL TAKE THE LEAD? WHAT WILL THE OTHER "TEACHER" DO?

Notes and Next Steps:

(Continued)

(Continued)

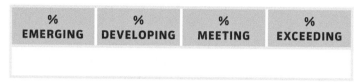

COACHING LOG: EVIDENCE OF TEACHER AND STUDENT LEARNING

Guiding Questions:

1. How did students perform on the post-assessment?

% EMERGING	% DEVELOPING	% MEETING	% EXCEEDING

2. What support will be given to students who did not meet the goal?
3. How have you grown professionally as a result of the coaching?
4. How can I continue to support you, even though the cycle is finished?

Notes and Next Steps:

Source: Sweeney, D. and Harris, L. (2020). *The Essential Guide for Student-Centered Coaching.* Reprinted with permission.

 Available for download from **resources.corwin.com/SCCFromaDistance**

Copyright © 2021 by Corwin Press, Inc. All rights reserved. Reprinted from *Student-Centered Coaching From a Distance: Coaching Moves for Virtual, Hybrid, and In-Person Classrooms* by Diane Sweeney, Leanna S. Harris. Thousand Oaks, CA: Corwin, www.corwin.com. Reproduction authorized for educational use by educators, local school sites, and/or noncommercial or nonprofit entities that have purchased the book.

Resource C

Planning Tools

Planner for Sharing Lessons

Learning Target:

WHAT'S HAPPENING? (LESSON COMPONENTS)	WHAT WILL IT LOOK LIKE?	WHO WILL TAKE THE LEAD? WHAT WILL THE OTHER "TEACHER" DO?

 Available for download from **resources.corwin.com/SCCFromaDistance**

Copyright © 2021 by Corwin Press, Inc. All rights reserved. Reprinted from *Student-Centered Coaching From a Distance: Coaching Moves for Virtual, Hybrid, and In-Person Classrooms* by Diane Sweeney, Leanna S. Harris. Thousand Oaks, CA: Corwin, www.corwin.com. Reproduction authorized for educational use by educators, local school sites, and/or noncommercial or nonprofit entities that have purchased the book.

Four-Square Planner

Whole-Group Instruction:

Focus of Instruction: **Students:**	**Focus of Instruction:** **Students:**
Focus of Instruction: **Students:**	**Focus of Instruction:** **Students:**

online resources ⌕ Available for download from **resources.corwin.com/SCCFromaDistance**

Copyright © 2021 by Corwin Press, Inc. All rights reserved. Reprinted from *Student-Centered Coaching From a Distance: Coaching Moves for Virtual, Hybrid, and In-Person Classrooms* by Diane Sweeney, Leanna S. Harris. Thousand Oaks, CA: Corwin, www.corwin.com. Reproduction authorized for educational use by educators, local school sites, and/or noncommercial or nonprofit entities that have purchased the book.

Resource D

Protocols and Agreements

TOOL: PROTOCOL FOR DETERMINING PRIORITY STANDARDS

1. Create grade or course-alike groups.

2. Provide the standards and ask participants to rank them using the rubric.

3. Regroup and discuss the rankings. Reach consensus on which are the highest-priority standards.

4. Unwrap each of the priority standards into a set of learning targets or success criteria.

TOOL: PROTOCOL FOR SORTING STUDENT WORK FROM A DISTANCE

Purpose: To analyze student evidence in order to plan for differentiated instruction.

Suggested time: 10–15 minutes

Process:

1. Be sure that both the coach and the teacher(s) have access to the set of work. It can be housed in the LMS or in a shared document. If working in person but still at a distance, it may make sense to create a copy of the set for each person.

2. Read through the entire set of class work, looking for trends relative to the learning target(s).

3. Discuss the trends that were noticed. Collectively, decide which ones are the most significant and need further instruction—either in whole or small groups.

4. Go back to the work to sort students according to the identified needs. If something pertains to the whole class, this will be addressed in whole-group instruction.

5. Plan for instruction based on the needs of each group.

TOOL: PROTOCOL FOR CO-PLANNING UNITS

1. Determine the goal or intended learning for the unit. Just like a coaching cycle goal, this can be framed as "Students will. . . ."

2. Unpack the learning intention into a set of learning targets ("I can . . ." statements). These targets will serve as the success criteria.

3. Plan the classwork, texts, and resources that will be needed to address each learning intention.

4. Plan how the learning intentions and/or learning targets will be assessed.

TOOL: PROTOCOL FOR CO-PLANNING LESSONS

1. Analyze the student work that came from previous instruction.

2. Based on the evidence, identify the learning target that will be focused on.

3. Determine what will happen synchronously and asynchronously.

4. Plan each lesson component.

5. Plan how students will show what they know. This includes how students will self-assess and how the teacher will formatively assess.

6. Determine how the students will be grouped for learning.

7. Practice the problems and tasks before teaching the lesson.

TOOL: PRINCIPAL AND COACH AGREEMENT

Principal:

Coach:

Date:

I. The Work

1. What is our focus for school improvement? How have student data informed this decision?

2. How will we demonstrate the impact of coaching on teacher and student learning?

II. Defining Our Roles

1. What roles and responsibilities will we each have in coaching and professional development?

2. How will we introduce the coaching role to the staff?

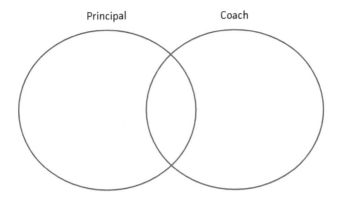

Principal   Coach

III. Ongoing Communication and Scheduling

1. When will we meet?

2. What will the coach's schedule look like? How will we provide choice to teachers?

3. How will we support each other?

TOOL: PARTNERSHIP AGREEMENT FOR A COACHING CYCLE

I. What Is Our Focus?

- What is our goal for student learning?

- What are the learning targets that capture what we want the students to know and be able to do?

II. How Will We Work Together?

- There are options for how we can work together in your classroom. Let's talk through these options and pick some that feel right to you.

- There are also options for how we can collect student evidence when we are working together in the classroom. How would you like to go about doing this?

- How will we reflect, both individually and collectively, about our work and students' growth?

III. How Will We Approach Co-planning?

- We will need at least 35 to 40 minutes each week for planning. What time works for you?

- It is helpful to create a planning system that works for you. How would you like to share this information (Google Docs, planning template, etc.)?

TOOL: STEPS FOR ENROLLING TEACHERS IN COACHING CYCLES

1. **Build Relationships by Connecting with Teachers in Person and Virtually**

   - Introduce yourself to the staff (whole staff, teams, and individuals) virtually and/or in person.
   - Help with various beginning-of-the-year tasks, such as classroom setup, technology, assessments, and so forth.
   - Provide resources to teachers for virtual and/or in-person teaching.

2. **Listen for Openings**

   - Find openings when coaching informally, such as co-planning lessons and units.
   - Attend existing meetings, such as PLCs, department meetings, or those for grade-level teams.
   - Invite teachers to participate, or ask if they will help you "practice" something new.

3. **Set Norms and Agreements**

   - Define clear expectations for the coach and teacher.
   - Discuss how you will best work together (this may vary, depending on whether it's happening virtually or in person).
   - Schedule times each week for co-planning and co-teaching.
   - If school shifts from remote to in person, or vice versa, plan how coaching will be adjusted.
   - Create a shared folder for all coaching documents, such as the Results-Based Coaching Tool and coaching logs.

4. **Launch Coaching Cycles**

Source: Adapted from Flaherty (2010).

TOOL: CONSULTANCY PROTOCOL

Purpose: This protocol is used to explore a problem or dilemma related to coaching.

Suggested time: 45 minutes

Roles:

- **Presenting coach** shares a dilemma for the group to discuss.
- **Participants** listen, reflect, and discuss the dilemma that is shared.
- **Facilitator** manages the process, keeps an eye on the time, and encourages everyone to participate in the discussion.

Process:

1. The presenter shares an issue or dilemma from their coaching work. If possible, the issue is presented in the form of a focus question (3–5 minutes).

2. The facilitator restates the issue or dilemma to ensure that it is clear and well understood (1–2 minutes).

3. Participants ask clarifying questions to be sure they understand the context and history of the issue or dilemma. The presenting coach responds to the questions to provide more context and background (5 minutes). (*Note:* Clarifying questions are aimed at helping the participants understand the issue or dilemma and are not a place to make suggestions.)

4. Participants ask probing questions. The presenting coach responds to the group's questions to continue adding context and background (5–10 minutes). (*Note:* Probing questions are deeper than clarifying questions but still are not suggestions. They are intended to spur reflection and possibility thinking.)

5. The presenting coach listens and takes notes while the participants discuss the issue or dilemma that was presented (5–10 minutes).

6. The presenting coach responds to the discussion and thoughtfully reflects on their next steps (5 minutes).

Source: Adapted from the National School Reform Faculty.

TOOL: PROTOCOL FOR PROVIDING STRENGTHS-BASED FEEDBACK

Purpose: This protocol is used to explore a problem or dilemma related to coaching.

Suggested time: 45 minutes

Roles:

- **Presenting coach** shares a dilemma for the group to discuss.
- **Participants** listen, reflect, and discuss the dilemma that is shared.
- **Facilitator** manages the process, keeps an eye on the time, and encourages everyone to participate in the discussion.

Process:

1. **Review the Protocol and Norms (5 minutes)**

   - The facilitator sets the stage for the learning and shares the following norms:

     ○ Assume positive intent throughout the conversation.

     ○ Listen and take notes.

     ○ Follow the protocol so that the conversation stays on track.

(Continued)

(Continued)

2. **Share a Problem of Practice (10 minutes)**

   - The presenting coach provides background about their recent coaching work.

   - The presenting coach shares a pressing challenge or issue.

   - Participants ask clarifying questions, so that the fuller picture is understood.

3. **Value (5 minutes)**

   - A few participants celebrate something they heard from the presenting coach.

4. **Uncover Possibilities (15 minutes)**

   - The presenting coach and participants brainstorm ideas that will support the coach in moving the work forward.

 Available for download from **resources.corwin.com/SCCFromaDistance**

Copyright © 2021 by Corwin Press, Inc. All rights reserved. Reprinted from *Student-Centered Coaching From a Distance: Coaching Moves for Virtual, Hybrid, and In-Person Classrooms* by Diane Sweeney, Leanna S. Harris. Thousand Oaks, CA: Corwin, www.corwin.com. Reproduction authorized for educational use by educators, local school sites, and/or noncommercial or nonprofit entities that have purchased the book.

Resource E

Tools for Self-Assessment

Self-Assessment Rubric

Intended Learning:

LEARNING TARGET	NOT THERE YET *Options for support:*	MEETS THE TARGET *Student provides evidence of meeting the learning target(s)* **What it looks like to meet the target:**	EXCEEDS THE TARGET *Student provides evidence of exceeding the learning target(s)*
I can...			
I can...			
I can...			

online resources Available for download from **resources.corwin.com/SCCFromaDistance**

Copyright © 2021 by Corwin Press, Inc. All rights reserved. Reprinted from *Student-Centered Coaching From a Distance: Coaching Moves for Virtual, Hybrid, and In-Person Classrooms* by Diane Sweeney, Leanna S. Harris. Thousand Oaks, CA: Corwin, www.corwin.com. Reproduction authorized for educational use by educators, local school sites, and/or noncommercial or nonprofit entities that have purchased the book.

Self-Assessment Checklist

Intended Learning:

LEARNING TARGET	NOT YET *I need to practice or get help. I can get there by:*	ALMOST THERE *I just need a little more practice. I can get there by:*	YES! *I'm there, and here's my evidence:*
I can . . .			
I can . . .			
I can . . .			

online resources ⌐ Available for download from **resources.corwin.com/SCCFromaDistance**

Copyright © 2021 by Corwin Press, Inc. All rights reserved. Reprinted from *Student-Centered Coaching From a Distance: Coaching Moves for Virtual, Hybrid, and In-Person Classrooms* by Diane Sweeney, Leanna S. Harris. Thousand Oaks, CA: Corwin, www.corwin.com. Reproduction authorized for educational use by educators, local school sites, and/or noncommercial or nonprofit entities that have purchased the book.

Resource F

Language for Coaching

TOOL: LANGUAGE THAT CREATES A SENSE OF BELONGING AMONG STUDENTS

- When you envision your classroom community, what do you hope it will feel like for each of your students?
- What specific steps will you take to engage students who haven't felt a sense of belonging in school?
- If school is held virtually or on a hybrid schedule, how will you build community so that all students feel connected?
- How will each student's voice be invited, honored, and valued by you and fellow students?
- What norms will be created and monitored to ensure that the students' voices are heard and honored?
- What routines will you create to allow all students to participate in the classroom community?
- As the coach, how can I support you in creating this community with your students?

TOOL: LANGUAGE FOR DETERMINING PRIORITY STANDARDS

- Let's look at the standards and decide which one is most relevant for your learners right now.
- Do we have any student evidence that could provide insights into what the students need?
- If we were to map the year, would this standard be revisited or only taught once?
- Is this standard used in more than one curricular area?
- Is this prerequisite learning for a future concept?

(Continued)

- Is this learning for all your students or a smaller group within your class?

- If you had to choose what matters most, what would it be?

- By the end of the year, what do you feel is most important for your students to know and do?

TOOL: LANGUAGE FOR GAINING CLARITY

- What is the intended learning for this unit or lesson? What standard(s) does it address?

- What will it look like if students are successful in this learning?

- How can students demonstrate their understanding, either digitally or in person?

- Is there anecdotal evidence we can collect?

- What is the purpose of the work students are creating? How will it be used?

- If students are receiving feedback, will it be descriptive or evaluative (such as a letter grade)?

TOOL: LANGUAGE FOR STAYING ASSET-BASED WHEN LOOKING AT STUDENT EVIDENCE

IF I HEAR OR NOTICE...	THEN I CAN SAY OR DO...
A teacher says, "I don't know what kind of math these kids learned in their home country, but they sure don't get the way we do it here."	You can respond, "It's so fascinating that sometimes different approaches and strategies are taught in different countries. I wonder if we could ask them to show their approach in a Flipgrid to the rest of the class. That would give us insight into what they already know, and it might give the other kids some new ways of approaching the problem. It would also give these newcomers a great way to shine."
When looking at student work, a teacher complains that a student doesn't know "anything" about the concept that's being taught.	You can remind the teacher that all kids come to school with a variety of schema and that part of our job is to uncover what they already know and to build on their strengths.
A teacher says, "I just get depressed looking at my students' work because it's a reminder of how far behind they are and how much ground I have to try to make up with them."	You might say, "Even though many students in your class are below grade level, it will be helpful to figure out what each one is bringing to the learning. That way, we can address the specific things they each need, which will help accelerate their learning."

TOOL: LANGUAGE FOR KEEPING PLANNING CONVERSATIONS FOCUSED ON LEARNING

IF I HEAR OR NOTICE ...	THEN I CAN SAY OR DO ...
When engaged in planning conversations, teachers immediately share activities that they found online.	Begin by thanking the teachers for researching and sharing their lesson ideas. Then nudge the conversation by saying, "What if we create a list of the learning targets? Then we can come up with some fun ideas for lessons. This way we'll be sure we are aligned with the standard."
Teachers aren't on the same page with their units. This is creating variations in the level of rigor that students are experiencing from classroom to classroom.	Meet with the principal to determine how to pull teachers together to do some unit planning. It would be up to the principal to frame why this is important and what the expectations are for teachers.
Sometimes it's hard to keep up in coaching conversations, and it feels embarrassing to ask someone to repeat themselves. This is especially hard when meetings are online.	Use a protocol for lesson and unit planning. This will provide a structure for the planning conversations. This can be as simple as a series of questions to guide you through the process.

TOOL: LANGUAGE FOR CO-PLANNING

- What needs to be in place so that every student can be successful in this lesson?
- Do we anticipate any misconceptions among students? If so, how will they be addressed?
- In what aspects of the lesson should scaffolds be added?
- In what aspects of the lesson should scaffolds be removed?
- How will we support language development?
- How will students demonstrate understanding?
- What student evidence can we use for the next planning session?

TOOL: LANGUAGE FOR CO-ASSESSING

Noticing and Naming	"Which learning target would you like me to focus on when I'm collecting student evidence?"
	"What points in the lesson will allow us to collect the most evidence?"

(Continued)

	"Is there any specific language you'd like me to listen for?" "Have we planned enough opportunities for the students to demonstrate what they know using the available technology?"
You Pick Four	"Are there any specific students you'd like me to focus on when I'm Noticing and Naming?" "Can you tell me more about these students?" "Would you like me to listen in during whole-group, small-group, or one-on-one instruction?" "Let's be sure we come together to co-plan after I collect this evidence."
Co-conferring	"There's so much we can learn by doing conferences together. How about if I join you in some, so that we can really get a good sense of where your students are in their learning?" "What learning target would you like to focus on?" "How can we structure the conversation so that it's both efficient and informative?" "How would you like to take notes during the conferences?"

TOOL: LANGUAGE FOR CO-DELIVERING LESSONS

Thinking Aloud	"I noticed ____. What I'm thinking is ____." "I think we might want to ____." "I'm wondering about ____." "When I see ____, it makes me think ____."
Teaching in Tandem	"What would you like to teach together?" "What parts of the lesson should each of us deliver?" When teaching online: "How can we use technology during the lesson?" "What if we ____?"
Micro Modeling	"I'm happy to micro model that part of the lesson. What pieces would you like to teach?" "I value what you bring to the lesson. Let's start there." When teaching online: "Can you tell me a little more about the videos we need to create for this unit?" When teaching online: "Are there tech tricks you need modeled? Like using breakout rooms or other features?"

TOOL: LANGUAGE FOR COACHING INTO SELF-ASSESSMENT

- Let's be sure we are crystal clear on what we want students to know and do and that we state everything in a way that students can understand on their own.

- How will we share the learning intention and success criteria with students?

- What kinds of supports need to be in place for students who aren't there yet on a target?

- What would we hope to see from students who have met each of the targets? Do we want to create exemplars for this?

TOOL: LANGUAGE FOR COACHING INTO DEEP LEARNING

IF I HEAR...	THEN I CAN SAY OR DO...
"I found this fun activity on Teachers Pay Teachers. I think the kids are really going to love it!"	"This definitely looks like a lot of fun, and our students need that right now with being stuck at home. Let's look at this checklist to see if the activity has the qualities we would want to see, so that we can be sure it's asking them to do some deep thinking and problem solving."
"I'm really struggling to keep up with this hybrid learning format, so I'll add some easy lessons to the LMS to keep the virtual learning students busy while I'm teaching the students who are face-to-face."	"Wow, concurrent instruction is really demanding a lot, and I appreciate all the hard work you're putting in. Maybe if the two of us can partner and work together on this, I can help you structure some meaningful learning for the asynchronous portion. That will help keep kids challenged and engaged, and they will come to the in-school lessons with you even better prepared."
"I know it's important to get kids to "struggle," but I worry about my students who will be doing this work on their own at home. They have such low skills, and I just don't know if they can handle it."	"I know how much you care about your students, and I agree that we need to give them work that they are capable of doing on their own without getting too overwhelmed and throwing in the towel. How about we look at some of these problem-solving tasks that are open-ended and have multiple entry points? That would allow all kids to access the material but still be challenged at their own level."

TOOL: LANGUAGE FOR DEFINING COACHING RIGHT NOW

IF WE HEAR OR NOTICE...	THEN THE PRINCIPAL CAN SAY OR DO...
The coach is teaching two sections of ELA to keep class sizes low. This has led many teachers to believe that the coach is no longer coaching. They are asking her to do all sorts of things, from covering classes to distributing hand sanitizer to classrooms.	The principal can explain to the staff that the coach is taking on these teaching duties temporarily, and the expectation is that the rest of the coach's time will be spent coaching.
Teachers are reaching out to the coach for a lot of tech help, but no one seems interested in moving into deeper work.	The principal may say, "Our coach has been spending a lot of time helping you get comfortable with the LMS, which has been a great asset. Don't forget that he's also available for mini and full coaching cycles. Many of you seem ready to jump into that, so be sure to let him know if you're interested."
Teachers are working hard to figure out how to deliver high-quality instruction online, but many are finding it to be a challenge. Because they feel so vulnerable and stressed, few have thought to reach out to the coach for help.	The principal may say, "I know it's hard to imagine how our coach could partner with you in a virtual lesson, but she was just sharing some of her experiences with me yesterday, and it sounds really powerful. Definitely reach out to her if you want to learn more."

TOOL: LANGUAGE FOR PARTNERING WITH A TEACHER

- Would you like to co-plan a lesson or unit or engage in a mini coaching cycle?

- What learning will we focus on?

- Is this being taught synchronously or asynchronously?

- Is there anything you want me to know about your students, circumstances, and so on?

- Is there anyone else you'd like to include in the work (special ed, ELL, district coach, tech coach)?

TOOL: LANGUAGE FOR PARTNERING WITH ANOTHER COACH

- As a district coach, how can I collaborate with the coaching that's happening in your school?

- I would like to coordinate with you and the principal to make sure we're all on the same page. When would be a good time to join one of your meetings?

- How can we support each other's coaching work?

- What is your plan for messaging coaching? Is there a way to include both of us in this?

- When does it make sense to partner in a cycle?

- What is our plan for communication?

 Available for download from **resources.corwin.com/SCCFromaDistance**

Copyright © 2021 by Corwin Press, Inc. All rights reserved. Reprinted from *Student-Centered Coaching From a Distance: Coaching Moves for Virtual, Hybrid, and In-Person Classrooms* by Diane Sweeney, Leanna S. Harris. Thousand Oaks, CA: Corwin, www.corwin.com. Reproduction authorized for educational use by educators, local school sites, and/or noncommercial or nonprofit entities that have purchased the book.

Resource G

Checklists for Coaching

TOOL: HOW HAVE I BEEN SPENDING MY TIME AS A COACH?

As you consider your coaching practice, how balanced has your work been? Put a check next to the statements that represent how you have been mostly spending your time as a coach. If you have more than a few checks, you may be ready to move beyond being a resource provider.

- ❑ I am mostly helping teachers with support, such as organizing assessments or other clerical duties.
- ❑ I am mostly helping teachers get technology systems in place.
- ❑ I am mostly engaged in conversations that are one-shot or drive-by.
- ❑ I am mostly working behind the scenes to write lessons and units for the teachers.
- ❑ I am mostly covering classes so that my school can manage cohorts of students.

TOOL: THINGS TO KEEP IN MIND WHEN CO-PLANNING

- ❑ Look for evidence that's easy to collect and analyze. This should be a quick process.
- ❑ Make sure the evidence is aligned with the designated outcome for learning.
- ❑ Keep an asset-based perspective. Focus on what kids already know, so that you can build from there.
- ❑ When co-planning instruction, think of what each student will need in order to be successful.
- ❑ Consider various ways in which students can demonstrate learning, especially in digital platforms.

TOOL: STRATEGIES FOR BEING PRODUCTIVE IN TECH-BASED CO-PLANNING SESSIONS

- ❑ Mix standing and sitting during co-planning sessions.
- ❑ Tell the teacher(s) that you may not focus on the camera because you will be capturing the conversation in a coaching log.
- ❑ Avoid multitasking.
- ❑ Turn off onscreen notifications.
- ❑ Hide "self-view" so that you don't watch yourself.
- ❑ Always schedule movement breaks between calls.
- ❑ Stay hydrated, and don't forget the snacks!

TOOL: CHECKLIST FOR WAYFINDING

- ❑ How easily can the students navigate the unit?
- ❑ Is the format of the unit consistent?
- ❑ Are the icons consistent from class to class and across the school and district?
- ❑ Is there a logical flow and structure to the lessons?
- ❑ Does the ease of navigation take students into deep learning?
- ❑ Do any of the lessons need to be tested or practiced?
- ❑ Can we use colors or images to support students?

TOOL: PLANNING BREAKOUT ROOMS

- ❑ How will we group students in breakout rooms?
- ❑ Is there a protocol that might help the groups stay on track?
- ❑ Are there any guiding questions we might use to frame the group work?
- ❑ How will we build in accountability for the group work?
- ❑ How long will the breakout rooms last?
- ❑ Can I help you organize and manage the breakout rooms?
- ❑ Which of the rooms will we visit?
- ❑ Is there another tool we can use to collect thinking (Padlet, Google Docs, Pear Deck, etc.)?
- ❑ Is there anything else I can help you with?

TOOL: COACHING TOWARD INDEPENDENCE

Coaches can support teachers in doing the following:

- ❑ Determine what learning needs to be scaffolded or, conversely, when too many scaffolds are in place.
- ❑ Create rituals and routines that provide students with the space to dig in first and, if needed, get help based on their specific needs.
- ❑ Model strategies to get unstuck. These may vary across face-to-face and remote learning environments.
- ❑ Use the Noticing and Naming strategy to watch for students who are struggling or stuck in a way that is no longer productive.
- ❑ Plan assignments that are challenging but also include the right number of scaffolds.
- ❑ Model language that promotes risk taking and a growth mindset.

TOOL: CHECKLIST FOR ASSESSING WHETHER TASKS LEAD TO DEEP LEARNING

- ❑ Students can think and solve problems in more than one way.
- ❑ Students are asked to share the strategies they used as learners.
- ❑ Information is applied in some way.
- ❑ Students are asked to think first.
- ❑ Students are able to decide how to approach the learning.

online resources ⟋ Available for download from **resources.corwin.com/SCCFromaDistance**

Copyright © 2021 by Corwin Press, Inc. All rights reserved. Reprinted from *Student-Centered Coaching From a Distance: Coaching Moves for Virtual, Hybrid, and In-Person Classrooms* by Diane Sweeney, Leanna S. Harris. Thousand Oaks, CA: Corwin, www.corwin.com. Reproduction authorized for educational use by educators, local school sites, and/or noncommercial or nonprofit entities that have purchased the book.

References

Bailey, K., & Jakicic, C. (2012). *Common formative assessment: A toolkit for professional learning communities at work.* Bloomington, IN: Solution Tree Press.

Boaler, J. (2016). *Mathematical mindsets: Unleashing students' potential through creative math, inspiring messages, and innovative teaching.* San Francisco, CA: Jossey-Bass.

California Department of Education. (2020). *Asset-based pedagogies.* Retrieved from https://www.cde.ca.gov/pd/ee/asset basedpedagogies.asp

Darling-Hammond, L., Hyler, M. E., & Gardner, M. (2017). *Effective teacher professional development.* Palo Alto, CA: Learning Policy Institute.

Donohoo, J. (2017). *Collective efficacy: How educators' beliefs impact student learning.* Thousand Oaks, CA: Corwin.

Fisher, D., Frey, N., & Hattie, J. (2020). *The distance learning playbook: Teaching for engagement and impact in any setting.* Thousand Oaks, CA: Corwin.

Flaherty, J. (2010). *Coaching: Evoking excellence in others* (3rd ed.). New York, NY: Routledge.

Fosslien, L., & Duffy, M. W. (2020, April 29). How to combat Zoom fatigue. *Harvard Business Review.* Retrieved from https://hbr.org/2020/04/how-to-combat-zoom-fatigue

Frey, N., & Fisher, D. (2013). *Rigorous reading.* Thousand Oaks, CA: Corwin.

Gonzalez, J. (2015, June 10). Dogfooding: How often do you do your own assignments? *Cult of Pedagogy.* Retrieved from https://www.cultofpedagogy.com/dogfooding

Hammond, Z. (2015). *Culturally responsive teaching and the brain: Promoting authentic engagement and rigor among culturally and linguistically diverse students.* Thousand Oaks, CA: Corwin.

Hattie, J. (2019, June). *Visible Learning: 250+ influences on student achievement.* Retrieved from https://us.corwin.com/sites/default/files/250_influences_chart_june_2019.pdf

Killion, J., Bryan, C., & Clifton, H. (2020). *Coaching matters* (2nd ed.). Oxford, OH: Learning Forward.

Krum, A. (2020, August 31). My daughter's learning disabilities fall between the cracks in Google Classroom. *ADDitude Magazine.* Retrieved from https://www.additudemag.com/online-hurdles-learning-disabilities-adhd

Matsumura, L., Sartoris, M., Bickel, D., & Garnier, H. (2009). Leadership for literacy coaching: The principal's role in launching a new coaching program. *Educational Administration Quarterly, 45*(5), 655–693.

McTighe, J. and Silver, H. (2020). Instructional shifts to support deep learning. *Educational Leadership Online.* https://www.educationalleadership-digital.com/educationalleadership/202009/MobilePagedArticle.action?articleId=1613225#articleId1613225

Minor, C. (2019). *We got this: Equity, access, and the quest to be who our students need us to be.* Portsmouth, NH: Heinemann.

O'Connell, M. J., & Vandas, K. (2015). *Partnering with students: Building ownership of learning.* Thousand Oaks, CA: Corwin.

Reeves, A. (2011). *Where great teaching begins: Planning for student thinking and learning.* Alexandria, VA: ASCD.

Spencer, J. (2020). *The power of student check-ins during distant learning and hybrid courses.* Retrieved from http://www.spencerauthor.com/student-check-ins/?utm_source=feedburner&

utm_medium=feed&utm_campaign=
Feed:+JohnSpencersBlog+(John+Spencer+
(@spencerideas))

Sweeney, D., & Harris, L. (2017). *Student-centered coaching: The moves.* Thousand Oaks, CA: Corwin.

Sweeney, D., & Harris, L. (2020). *The essential guide for student-centered coaching.* Thousand Oaks, CA: Corwin.

Townsley, M., & Knight, M. (2020). 3 big shifts for standards-based grades. *ASCD Express,* 16(2).

Wiliam, D. (2011). *Embedded formative assessment.* Bloomington, IN: Solution Tree Press.

Zweig, D. (2014, June 12). How to know where you're going when you're in an airport. *The Atlantic.* Retrieved from https://www.theatlantic.com/business/archive/2014/06/how-you-know-where-youre-going-when-youre-in-an-airport/372537

Index

A SAGE Publishing Company

Helping educators make the greatest impact

CORWIN HAS ONE MISSION: to enhance education through intentional professional learning.

We build long-term relationships with our authors, educators, clients, and associations who partner with us to develop and continuously improve the best evidence-based practices that establish and support lifelong learning.

Keep learning...

Also from Diane Sweeney

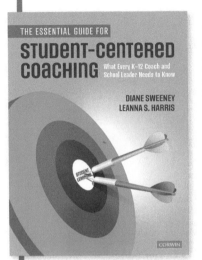

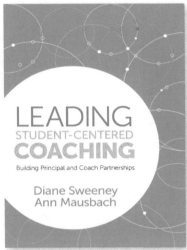

Available for consulting!

Diane Sweeney

Leanna Harris

Diane Sweeney Consulting supports the implementation of Student-Centered Coaching in K–12 schools. Student-Centered Coaching introduces a new way of delivering instructional coaching that puts the needs of students' front and center. By focusing coaching on goals for student learning, rather than on fixing teachers, an instructional coach can directly impact instructional practice and student achievement.

For more information, visit **www.dianesweeney.com**

DIANESWEENEYCONSULTING
THE PLACE FOR STUDENT-CENTERED COACHING

CORWIN

LDN21156